CUBA

BY TAMMY GAGNE

Essential Library
An Imprint of Abdo Publishing
abdobooks.com

ABDOBOOKS.COM

Published by Abdo Publishing, a division of ABDO, PO Box 398166, Minneapolis, Minnesota 55439. Copyright © 2026 by Abdo Consulting Group, Inc. International copyrights reserved in all countries. No part of this book may be reproduced in any form without written permission from the publisher. Essential Library™ is a trademark and logo of Abdo Publishing.

Printed in China.
052025
092025

 THIS BOOK CONTAINS RECYCLED MATERIALS

Cover Photo: Feifei Cui-Paoluzzo/Moment/Getty Images; iStock/Getty Images (pattern)
Interior Photos: Richie Chan/Shutterstock Images, 4–5, 12, 70–71; Sven Creutzmann/Mambo Photography/Getty Images News/Getty Images, 9; Shutterstock Images, 10, 14–15, 16 (bottom), 19, 20, 24, 31, 43, 52–53, 54–55, 61, 64, 74, 77, 82, 84, 86–87, 95, 96, 99; Red Line Editorial, 16 (top); Created by Tomas Zrna/Moment/Getty Images, 23; Rostislav Ageev/Shutterstock Images, 26–27; Komkrit Preechachanwate/Shutterstock Images, 28; Piotr Poznan/Shutterstock Images, 32; Bernard Radvaner/Corbis/Getty Images, 34–35; David Keep/Shutterstock Images, 37; Emily Marie Wilson/Shutterstock Images, 38–39; John Carter Brown Library, 40; The Spanish and American Illustration XVI, 45; Bettmann/Getty Images, 46; STR/AFP/Getty Images, 49; Rafiq Maqbool/AP Images, 51; Elena Veselova/Shutterstock Images, 58; George Rinhart/Corbis Historical/Getty Images, 60; Vladimir Wrangel/Shutterstock Images, 62; Maarten Zeehandelaar/Shutterstock Images, 63; Kako Escalona/Shutterstock Images, 67; Carlos Gonzalez Ximenez/Shutterstock Images, 68–69; Maurizio Bersanelli/Shutterstock Images, 72; Yamil Lage/AFP/Getty Images, 80–81; Emily Marie Wilson/Shutterstock Images, 88; Predrag Jankovic/Shutterstock Images, 89; Kuznetsov Alexey/Shutterstock Images, 90–91; Neslihan Gorucu/Shutterstock Images, 101

Editor: Kari Cornell
Series Designer: Maggie Villaume

Library of Congress Control Number: 2024948555

PUBLISHER'S CATALOGING-IN-PUBLICATION DATA

Names: Gagne, Tammy, author.
Title: Cuba / by Tammy Gagne
Description: Minneapolis, Minnesota: Abdo Publishing, 2026 | Series: Essential library of countries | Includes online resources and index.
Identifiers: ISBN 9781098296964 (lib. bdg.) | ISBN 9798384919483 (ebook)
Subjects: LCSH: Geography--Juvenile literature. | Cuba--Juvenile literature. | Islands of the Caribbean--Juvenile literature. | Cuba--History--Juvenile literature.
Classification: DDC 917.291--dc23

CONTENTS

CHAPTER ONE
A TOUR OF CUBA 4

CHAPTER TWO
GEOGRAPHY 14

CHAPTER THREE
PLANTS AND ANIMALS 26

CHAPTER FOUR
HISTORY 38

CHAPTER FIVE
PEOPLE AND CULTURE 52

CHAPTER SIX
POLITICS 70

CHAPTER SEVEN
ECONOMICS 80

CHAPTER EIGHT
CUBA TODAY 90

ESSENTIAL FACTS 100
GLOSSARY 102
ADDITIONAL RESOURCES 104
SOURCE NOTES 106
INDEX 110
ABOUT THE AUTHOR 112

CHAPTER ONE

A TOUR OF CUBA

Noah had been excited when he signed up for his high school's foreign language immersion program in Cuba, but nothing compared to the exhilaration he felt upon arriving at the José Martí International Airport in Havana, Cuba. It looked a bit old-fashioned but similar to airports in the United States. People rushed past Noah rolling suitcases along the tiled floor.

Many travelers split their attention between walking and searching for their gate numbers. But the conversations sounded much different than they had in Ohio, where Noah had begun his journey early that morning. His immersion in the Spanish language had already begun.

Havana, founded in 1519, became a center for the Caribbean's shipbuilding industry by the 1600s.

> The largest airport in Cuba, José Martí International Airport, serves four million travelers each year.[1]

Somewhere in the crowd near the baggage claim was Noah's host family, the people who were opening their home to him for the next several weeks. Noah had spent many months texting with one of the younger members of the Martinez family on CubaMessenger and sharing photos through the app. Like Noah, Alejandro was 16 years old. The two boys had already discovered they had much in common. They both loved food of every kind. Noah was especially excited to try flan, Alejandro's favorite dessert. And both boys were also big fans of the *Fast & Furious* movie series. One of the films was set in Cuba, but Noah hadn't known it was shot in Havana until Alejandro told him.

As Noah searched the luggage carousel for his bag, a hand clapped his shoulder. "¡Bienvenido a Cuba!" Alejandro said. Noah smiled as the Cuban teen welcomed him. "Come on," Alejandro said. "Mamá and Papá can't wait to meet you—and feed you. I told them you probably packed snacks for the plane ride."

"I did," Noah confessed, "but I ate them all."

"Please tell me you are hungry," Alejandro implored. "Mamá has been cooking all morning for an early *almuerzo*." Noah knew from his Spanish lessons that this word meant "lunch."

"Oh, I could definitely eat again," he replied.

The boys shared a laugh as they worked their way through the crowd to find Alejandro's parents.

> **ENGLISH REQUIREMENTS**
>
> Although English has been taught in some Cuban schools since 1899, the Cuban government began requiring students to learn the language in 2016. That same year, the first graduating class of English teachers began their new jobs in school systems across the country. Cuban children take English classes beginning in the lower grades. Later, they must demonstrate a proficiency in the language as one of their secondary school graduation requirements. Being able to speak English is considered important for success in many business settings around the world, so the Cuban government prioritized it as key to growing the nation's economy.

At the Martinez home, Noah was treated to one of the best meals of his life. Mrs. Martinez had prepared *ropa vieja*, Cuba's national dish, to celebrate his arrival. She had slow-cooked the beef in a flavorful tomato sauce and served it shredded over rice with black beans on the side.

As the family ate, Alejandro's father shared the legend behind the popular meal. The name *ropa vieja* translates to "old clothes" in Spanish. It is said to be the creation of a man who did not have enough money to buy food for his family. According to the story, the man shredded his own clothing to feed his loved ones. He prayed as he cooked the tattered fabric and watched it miraculously transform into a delicious stew.

OLD HAVANA

After lunch, Noah joined the Martinez family for a guided tour of Old Havana, a historic district in the city. Noah was enjoying the charm of walking the cobblestone streets while learning about history. Alejandro's little sisters, Marisol and Sofia, were as excited about the activity as Noah was.

At nine years old, the twin girls were still learning about their nation's history. Alejandro had already learned much of Cuba's history in school, so he was more focused on the rest of the afternoon. He told Noah, "We have something even more fun planned for later."

The tour began at the Plaza de Armas, the center square of the city that was founded in 1515. This part of Havana was often used to conduct military exercises. Many of the buildings in the square dated back to the late 1700s. In 1834, a statue of Spanish monarch Ferdinand VII stood in this area, but the guide told the group that in 1955 it had been replaced with the marble statue of Carlos Manuel de Céspedes that now stood before them. Céspedes initiated Cuba's fight for independence from Spain in the late 1800s. An abolitionist, Céspedes was elected president by the revolutionary government in 1869.

Even the Martinez family was surprised by how much there was to see and learn on the tour. As the group moved toward the Cathedral of Havana, Noah and the others walked on a wooden street. The guide explained that it was created in the 1830s when many streets were made of dirt or paved with stone. The wood offered two main advantages. First, it didn't become muddy after rain. Second, it was quieter than paving stones when horse-drawn carriages traveled through the area. Now only

ROPA VIEJA'S TRUE ORIGIN

Recipes for ropa vieja are said to go back at least 500 years. The dish has been traced to Sephardic Jews on Spain's Iberian Peninsula. Their religion does not allow the Sephardi people to cook on the Sabbath, their day of rest each week, so many people slow-cook ropa vieja the day before. The dish became popular in Cuba when the island was colonized by Spain in the 1500s.

The Plaza de Armas has been carefully restored to maintain the architecture and style of the Spanish colonial era.

pedestrians are allowed to cross La Calle de Madera, which means "the wooden street" in Spanish. This is because wood wears down much faster than cobblestones.

In the Plaza de la Catedral, Noah and his host family encountered a variety of talented people. Artisans sold crafts near the historic church. Street performers played live music in the square. Marisol and Sofia began dancing to the sounds of guitars, bongo drums, and maracas. The guide told the group that the music, which blended Spanish guitar music with African rhythms, was

Visitors and Cubans alike gather at the Plaza de la Catedral, which dates to the 1700s. They listen to traditional Cuban music, shop for arts and crafts, and watch street performers.

known as *son Cubano*. Noah took in all the sights and sounds, amazed by the cathedral's elaborate stonework, the powerful music, and the welcoming nature of the Cuban people. Seeing Noah experience Old Havana for the first time made Alejandro appreciate the city he often took for granted.

THE MUSEO DEL AUTOMÓVIL

When the tour ended, Alejandro revealed his big surprise for the rest of the afternoon. The family was taking Noah to the Museo del Automóvil. This automobile museum housed some of the oldest and most famous cars in the world. Some were once owned by well-known Cubans, and others were rare models from automotive history. Alejandro told Noah that his favorite car at the museum was the Cadillac used by Che Guevara, a major figure of the Cuban Revolution. He then added that the Model T, which launched Henry Ford's success in the American automotive industry in 1908, was also a sight to behold.

> There are approximately 60,000 antique US cars in Cuba.[2]

Alejandro had begun planning the trip to the museum when he and Noah first started chatting about cars. It was Noah's love for automobiles that sparked his interest in the *Fast & Furious* films. Noah had read that Cuba was a bit like an auto museum itself, where old US cars were a frequent sight on city streets. He admitted in a text that getting to see the cars in person was part of why he had chosen Cuba out of all the Spanish-speaking countries that offered language immersion programs.

It is no coincidence that Cuba is home to so many antique US cars. Cuba has never had its own car manufacturing industry. When cars first became common for the public to own in the early 1900s, Cuba began importing vehicles from the United States. But trade between the countries stopped for political reasons in the 1960s, ending car imports. This forced people who already owned a US car to get creative about its maintenance. Many of the antique cars still running on the streets used parts from Russia, since Cuba maintained trade with that country.

RESTING UP FOR DAY TWO

Noah and the Martinez family were exhausted when they returned home after the walking tour and museum visit. Noah thanked Alejandro's parents for making his first day in Cuba such an enjoyable one. They were pleased he had as much fun as they did. Mrs. Martinez told Noah she

Antique American cars are a popular mode of transportation in Old Havana. About 50 percent of the cars are from the 1950s.

would be in the kitchen cooking with Mr. Martinez if he needed her. He appreciated that she spoke slowly and clearly to help him understand everything she said in Spanish. He couldn't have ended up with a better host family.

The next day, Noah's language immersion class was going to a *fútbol* match with their teacher. Noah had grown up playing this sport, which is known as soccer in the United States. He was looking forward to experiencing the event with his fellow US students in this new nation he still had so much to learn about. But first, he needed some food and rest.

"Let's go see if there's any ropa vieja left," Alejandro suggested.

"Aren't your parents making dinner?" Noah asked him.

"Tell me you aren't worried about ruining your appetite," Alejandro scoffed.

> **TRAVELING FROM THE UNITED STATES TO CUBA**
>
> People from all over the world travel to Cuba for vacations. But US law prohibits Americans from traveling to the nation solely for tourism due to long-standing political differences between the two countries. US citizens may obtain a visa for specific purposes. These include family visits, religious activities, and educational opportunities. It's common for US citizens to travel to Cuba for foreign exchange student programs, academic research, and teaching jobs.

Noah then did exactly as Alejandro instructed but in Spanish. "*No estoy preocupado por arruinar mi apetito*," he said. Just as they had at the airport, the boys shared a laugh over their love of food before heading to the Martinez kitchen.

THE NATION OF CUBA

The country formally known as the Republic of Cuba is located on the island of Cuba, the largest island in the Caribbean Sea. After Haiti and the Dominican Republic, Cuba has the third-largest population of all the Caribbean nations.[3] Cuba has a long and complex history that includes Indigenous peoples, a Spanish colonial period, a revolutionary era, and the nation's establishment as a socialist state under Fidel Castro. The early 2000s marked a gradual reopening of the nation to the rest of the world after it had been closed off for decades under Castro.

Today the country is known for its beautiful beaches, delicious food and coffee, lively music, and many architectural styles. Cuba offers people a chance to experience many different aspects of its culture. Among the things visitors often enjoy most are the Carnival of Santiago de Cuba, live music and dance performances, and Cuban cuisine.

CHAPTER **TWO**

GEOGRAPHY

The Republic of Cuba is located at the intersection of three major bodies of water. The Atlantic Ocean is to Cuba's northeast, and the Gulf of Mexico is to the country's west. To Cuba's south lie the Caribbean Sea and nearly all the other countries of the Caribbean. The closest country to Cuba is Haiti, which is 48 miles (77 km) from Cuba's eastern shore.[1] Other close neighbors include the Bahamas, which is the only Caribbean nation to Cuba's north, and Jamaica to its south.

Cuba is an archipelago. It includes the main island of Cuba, the smaller Isla de la Juventud, and about 4,000 much smaller islands.[2] Cuba's land covers 42,402 square miles (109,820 sq km).[3] This is slightly smaller than the state of Pennsylvania. The main island makes up most of the nation. Isla de la Juventud lies about 60 miles

Varadero Beach, located two hours east of Havana, is one of 430 beaches on the Cuban coast.

MAP OF
CUBA

KEY:
- 🟥 Capital
- ⚪ City
- 📍 Point of Interest

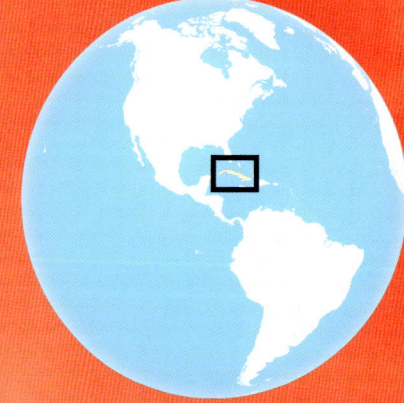

(97 km) south of the mainland. The country's largest offshore island, it covers 934 square miles (2,419 sq km).[4] This is about three-quarters the size of the state of Rhode Island.[5]

Cuba's land includes a variety of terrain. Dry forests once covered more than half the country. This is because much of the land has shallow soil that doesn't hold much water. As much as 90 percent of the forestland has now been harvested for its trees, however. As a result, the former dry forests have become savannas. The dry forests that remain in Cuba are found in the island's interior, from sea level up to about 2,297 feet (700 m) in elevation.[6] The vegetation consists mainly of evergreen species such as aguacatillo, jocuma, and macurije trees.

Moist forests are found in many parts of Cuba. They also cover a range of elevations, from lowland forests to mountain rainforests. In lowland forests, crabwood and acana trees grow. Some species in these areas reach heights of up to 131 feet (40 m). Yellow oliver and cuajaní trees are found in the higher elevations. These trees typically reach about 98 feet (30 m).[7] Most of the rainforests in the country remain untouched. This is because the mountainous land is of little use for agriculture and is difficult to develop for other uses.

Many of Cuba's grasslands are found in the nation's six biosphere reserves. These areas are part of the United Nations Educational, Scientific and Cultural Organization (UNESCO) Man and the Biosphere Programme. It aims to balance the relationship between people and the environment. UNESCO also helps preserve and protect historic lands and buildings because of their cultural significance. Grasslands are large open areas that serve as important resources. People depend on them for food and energy. Grasslands also serve as essential wildlife habitats.

Cuba's coastal areas include rugged mangrove forests and delicate coral reefs. Dense groups of mangrove trees and shrubs thrive in the intertidal zones. With much of their root systems exposed, mangroves look as if they are standing on stilts in the water. This strong framework helps mangrove trees withstand the continual pushing and pulling of the tides. Mangroves play a big role in protecting Cuba's coral reefs. These trees filter sediment and pollution before they reach the reefs and the marine life the reefs contain.

MOUNTAINS

The Sierra Maestra range is in southeastern Cuba. At 6,476 feet (1,974 m) above sea level, Pico Turquino is the tallest mountain peak in both this range and the nation.[8] The peak's name is based on the Spanish word *turquesa*, which means "turquoise." The Caribbean Sea, which becomes visible to hikers as they climb toward the summit, is known for this vibrant color.

A RECORD-SETTING DAY IN CUBA

On June 11, 2015, twin brothers Eric and Matthew Gilbertson became the first people to climb the highest mountain in all twenty-three North American countries. Making it to the top of Sierra Maestra's Pico Turquino put the young men from Berea, Kentucky, in the record books, as it was their final climb of the ambitious endeavor. The climbers began with Mount Denali in Alaska in May 2010, and it took them a little more than five years to complete their goal.

Another part of the Sierra Maestra is La Gran Piedra. This name means "great rock" in Spanish. La Gran Piedra is a huge volcanic rock. It measures 98 feet (30 m) wide, 167 feet (51 m) long, and 82 feet (25 m) high.[9] More than 400 stone steps lead visitors to the top, which sits 4,101 feet

The slopes of Pico Turquino and the other mountains in the Sierra Maestra are thick with mahogany, ebony, and cedar trees.

Water rushes over falls in Topes de Collantes park reserve.

(1,250 m) above sea level. This elevation is high enough for many people to see lights from Jamaica if they reach the top of Gran Piedra on a dark night.[10]

The Sierra Maestra region is known for its many coffee plantations. Coffee beans have long been farmed in the mountain regions of the country, where the volcanic soil provides ideal conditions for the beans to grow. Although Cuba now sells less coffee to other countries than it did in the past, most of the coffee exported from Cuba comes from the Sierra Maestra.

The oldest coffee plantations in Cuba date to the 1700s and have been recognized as UNESCO World Heritage sites. The architecture, irrigation systems, and mountain roads and bridges that connected the plantations were incredibly advanced for their time.

The Escambray Mountains form another major mountain range in Cuba. This one is located near the center of the country, stretching about 50 miles (80 km) east to west. Pico San Juan is this range's highest peak, at 3,150 feet (960 m).[11] The range is separated into two sections by the Agabama River. The Guamuhaya Mountains lie to the west, while the Sierra de Sancti Spíritus are found to the east. Visitors are often drawn to this region to see its variety of plants and animals as well as its many waterfalls.

COASTLINE AND MAJOR WATERWAYS

Cuba's many bays, inlets, and smaller islands give the country a long, irregular coastline. Its total length is approximately 3,570 miles (5,745 km).[12] The northern coast consists of low and somewhat rocky land. The southern coast is a mix of mountainous terrain and lowlands with more marshes.

Numerous rivers flow through Cuba and empty into the Caribbean Sea. The country's longest river is the Cauto in eastern Cuba, measuring 230 miles (370 km). Although only about 70 miles (113 km) of the river is wide and deep enough for ships to pass through it, the banks of the Cauto benefit greatly from the water it provides.[13] Water from the river is used to irrigate many important crops. Rice, citrus,

CUBA'S UNDERGROUND RIVERS AND CAVES

Many of Cuba's rivers have sections that travel underground. Over millions of years, water has broken down large parts of the country's bedrock, which is the hard material found beneath Earth's soil. This is because so much of Cuba's bedrock is made of limestone, which is easily dissolved by water. This process has created extensive underground river systems in Cuba, which include more than 3,000 caves.[14]

and sugarcane are just a few of the crops that grow in the Cauto River valley. Farmers also raise cattle on the banks of this important waterway.

The Toa River is nicknamed the Cuban Amazon. Although it is far from the longest waterway at just 81 miles (130 km), the Toa has 72 tributaries.[15] Its surrounding land and forests serve as a habitat for a variety of plants and animals, including many birds, insects, and reptiles. Like those of the Amazon River in South America, the Toa's nearby forests are incredibly dense. In many areas, sunlight doesn't reach parts of the forest floor.

Rocky cliffs as tall as 984 feet (300 m) surround the Yumurí River, which flows through Yumurí Canyon in eastern Cuba.[16] This river is even smaller than the Toa, measuring about 34 miles (55 km) long.[17] The beautiful scenery attracts many visitors to the canyon. They often travel the river by boat, hike along its banks, and even bathe in its waters.

> **Cuba has more than 500 rivers.**[19]

CLIMATE

Cuba has a tropical climate with two distinct seasons. Summer lasts from May until October, bringing high humidity and large amounts of rain. It rarely rains for hours at a time, however. Most storms are short and occur near the end of the day. The yearly rainfall averages between 40 and 60 inches (102–152 cm). The least amount of rain falls in the southernmost section of Cuba, which receives just 28 inches (70 cm) of rain annually.[18]

The Yumurí River flows through the Yumurí Canyon before it empties into the Straits of Florida along Cuba's northern coast.

When Hurricane Irma struck Cuba in 2017, it left flooded streets and damaged buildings in its wake. The storm killed at least ten people.

    The average air temperature in August is about 86 degrees Fahrenheit (30°C). The winter season begins in November and lasts until April. This season is drier and slightly cooler, with an average air temperature of 68 degrees Fahrenheit (20°C) in February. Even the seawater in Cuba remains relatively warm all year, reaching a high of 86 degrees Fahrenheit (30°C) in the summer and dipping only to about 75 degrees Fahrenheit (24°C) in the winter.[20]

    Hurricane season in Cuba runs from June through November, with most storms occurring in September and October. Because Cuba is an island nation, even the inland areas usually experience damaging winds and flooding from hurricanes. Heavy rain and storm surges can contribute to widespread flooding, reaching as far as a third of a mile (0.50 km) inland.[21] Some areas even experience mudslides and tornadoes during these storms. But Cuba has one of the best records for hurricane preparedness and response, which has saved many lives when storms have hit the nation.

In September 2022, Hurricane Ian struck Cuba's western coast. The category 3 storm brought winds moving as fast as 125 miles per hour (201 kmh), knocking out power for the entire island. This left more than 11 million people in the nation without electricity. As the storm moved toward Florida, many parts of Cuba flooded. The province of Pinar del Río was the hardest hit. Trees were uprooted, and buildings suffered devastating damage. At least five people were killed in the natural disaster.[22]

The effects of the storm could have been much worse. Experts credited Cuba's Civil Defense System, a network of early warnings, evacuation plans, and building codes that help keep the Cuban people safe when storms hit the island. It has proven effective even when stronger hurricanes make their way to Cuba.

HURRICANE MILTON

Cuba is often in the path of hurricanes, experiencing direct hits or the effects of about eight storms per year. On October 8, 2024, Hurricane Milton passed the northwestern Cuban coast, causing a storm surge and heavy rains that flooded streets in Havana. The most powerful storm ever to hit Cuba was Hurricane Irma in 2017. The category 5 storm brought winds as fast as 160 miles per hour (257 kmh).[23]

CHAPTER THREE

PLANTS AND ANIMALS

Cuba has a variety of plants and animals, many of which can be found only in this Caribbean nation. Some species have strong historical and cultural meaning. The white mariposa is Cuba's national flower. Because the word *mariposa* means "butterfly" in Spanish, this flower is also called the butterfly jasmine. It thrives in Cuba's humid climate, blooming between July and September.

This species, which has fragrant white petals, is loved for its beauty and pleasing scent, but the flower is also a symbol of the Cuban people's resilience. The white mariposa can grow in different types of soil, easily adapting to its environment. Although the plant grows well in the sun, it can grow in partial shade.

The coral reefs near Cuba's northern coast are teeming with yellow snappers and corals.

Cuban royal palms are native to Cuba, but they also grow in Hawaii and Florida.

> **THRIVING FLOWERS**
>
> Cuba has more than 300 species of orchids.[2] These plants grow well in the country's humid, tropical climate. Although many orchids look delicate, they are a surprisingly adaptable flower. They can grow directly from the soil, on other plants such as vines, or even on rocks. They also grow in both lowland and highland areas. Cuba's orchids can be found near the coast, on farmlands, and in wooded parts of the island.

The white mariposa has long been used in Cuban ceremonies and traditions. For example, because its color is also a symbol of purity, the flower is a common offering in some religious ceremonies. Because all parts of the white mariposa are edible, the flower is used in cooking too.

Perhaps the most unusual use of the flower, however, occurred during the Cuban Independence Movement between 1868 and 1898. Women of high social standing hid secret messages in the blooms and then gave the white mariposa flowers to rebel fighters. This usage gave the flower additional meanings of courage, resistance, and the hope for freedom.

CUBAN ROYAL PALM TREES

Palm trees can be found all over Cuba. One of the most common species is the Cuban royal palm, which can grow between 40 and 60 feet (12 and 18 m) tall. The smooth trunk narrows toward the top, where feathery leaves are up to 20 feet (6 m) long.[1] Like other vegetation in the Caribbean, Cuban royal palms thrive in humidity. They grow best in wide-open spaces such as Cuba's plains. The only places where they are not abundant are in the swampy regions of the country, as the species does not grow well in wetlands.

Nicknamed the queen of the fields, the Cuban royal palm has several useful parts. Hog farmers often plant royal palms on their land because the species produces an oil-rich fruit called *palmiche*, which the farmers feed to their animals. The trees' strong trunks are often used to make fence posts. Their leaf stems are used for making brooms. Not even the sheath of the leaves is wasted when a tree is harvested, as this part of the plant is used for making baskets.

ENDANGERED PLANT SPECIES

Another palm tree, the cork palm, is far less abundant in Cuba. This species, which has grown on the island for 100 million years, is now a rare sight largely due to deforestation. Today the tree is found only in western regions of Cuba. Smaller than the royal palm, the tallest cork palms grow to about 33 feet (10 m). It is estimated that only about 600 of these trees are left in Cuba, which is the only place they grow.[3] The tree is considered critically endangered. This means that it is at high risk of becoming extinct.

The West Indian walnut tree is also critically endangered in Cuba. Deforestation and forest fires have contributed to the decline of this species. Growing up to 82 feet (25 m) tall, the West Indian

CUBAN MAHOGANY

Before Spanish explorers arrived in Cuba, mahogany trees grew abundantly there. Wood from the trees was known for being strong but bendable as well as lightweight. These properties made Cuban mahogany a popular building material for ships and fine furniture. But soon the trees had been overharvested, with more of them being cut down than growing to maturity. In 1946, Cuba banned exports of the wood. Cuban mahogany is now a protected tree species in the country.

walnut has long been valued for its wood, which is ideal for building.[4] The tree also produces nuts, which many Cuban people consider a delicacy.

CUBAN TROGON

Cuba has nearly 400 bird species.[5] One of the most common is the Cuban trogon. Found only in Cuba, it lives in a variety of habitats, including dry and wet forests. Though the species prefers shade to sunlight, the birds can also be found in areas where most of the trees have been harvested.

The trogon is a colorful species. Its crown is blue, its throat and chest are white, its belly and beak are red, and its back is green. Several of these colors are also found on Cuba's flag, which led to the species being named the country's national bird.

Trogons usually measure between ten and 11 inches (25–28 cm) from the tips of their beaks

The Cuban trogon is nicknamed the tocororo or the tocoloro in Spanish, words that mimic the sound this species makes.

31

to the ends of their tails.[6] These birds typically nest in trees where other animals have already made spaces, such as in abandoned woodpecker holes. The trogon eats flowers, fruits, and insects. It is one of the few bird species that can hover over its food while eating it.

The Cuban people consider this bird a symbol of freedom because of its resistance to being domesticated. If a member of the species is placed in a cage, it will usually do everything in its power to escape, even banging its body against the bars. It will continue fighting against containment to the point of injury or death.

CUBAN SOLENODON

One of Cuba's most unusual animals is the Cuban solenodon. This shrew-like creature has a long, thin snout that it uses to find insects, spiders, earthworms, and scorpions to eat. It also feeds on fruits, leaves, and roots.

Most solenodons measure between 11 and 15 inches (28–38 cm) long and weigh about two pounds (1 kg).[7] This animal's body is covered with dark brown or black hair. It also has a long tail with scaly skin. Despite its small size, the solenodon is a dangerous predator. It attacks with a bite that injects venomous saliva. The venom quickly immobilizes the prey.

BEE HUMMINGBIRD

Cuba is home to the smallest bird in the world: the bee hummingbird. This species, which is found only in Cuba, measures just 2.4 inches (6 cm) long. It weighs less than 0.07 ounces (2 g), which is less than the weight of a dime.[8] Visitors to Alexander von Humboldt National Park in eastern Cuba often encounter this bird species, although many people mistake it for a bee because of the bird's tiny size.

The solenodon may go from the hunter to the hunted if it is discovered by a snake or bird of prey. Many solenodons have also been killed by domestic dogs and cats in areas where residential neighborhoods have taken over the solenodons' former habitat. Although a solenodon will try to protect itself with its venom, it typically burrows into the ground to avoid predators before it encounters them.

CORAL REEFS

Coral reefs are found in tropical and subtropical waters, including the Caribbean Sea. Hard corals are a species of invertebrate that live in the world's oceans along coastlines. The seawater helps them grow firm exoskeletons. These external coverings protect the corals from harm. Made of a chemical compound called calcium carbonate, the exoskeletons also create a habitat for many other marine species.

As generations of corals live and die, their exoskeletons remain in the water, creating a structure that is many layers deep. New coral colonies build on the older generations, increasing the size of the coral reef over time. Although coral reefs are porous, they are also strong. Still, they can be destroyed if they are not protected from people. Many of these underwater ecosystems in the Caribbean and beyond are endangered. Pollution and climate change have damaged many coral reef systems, but Cuba's coral reefs are doing much better than most others.

The elkhorn coral species, for example, has almost disappeared from the Florida Keys in the United States. The US Endangered Species Act lists this type of coral as a threatened

Jardines de la Reina is a protected marine park off the southeastern coast of Cuba. It has staghorn, elkhorn, and black corals, some of which are more than 4,000 years old.

species throughout its natural habitat. The International Union for Conservation of Nature (IUCN) Red List classifies it as critically endangered. On Cuba's coastline, however, elkhorn coral are thriving. This is because Cuba has the largest marine reserve in the Caribbean.

The country has protected about 23 percent of its shallow waters.[9] Cuba bans fishing in certain places, which keeps the predators and prey in good balance. Cuban farmers do not use as many chemicals as growers in other nations. This has reduced the pollution that flows into the sea with rainwater. The nation also doesn't have many homes or other buildings along its coastline, further reducing coastal pollution.

As a result of these efforts, many marine species that live within Cuba's coral reefs are also thriving. These include crabs, scallops, and sea urchins. The effects of these healthy reefs extend to larger species that inhabit nearby waters. Sharks, which are threatened or endangered in many other parts of the world, are abundant in the waters off Cuba because their food is so plentiful in these areas.

ENDANGERED ANIMAL SPECIES

While some of Cuba's conservation efforts have been successful, there are animal species in the nation that are struggling. The Cuban crocodile is one of the most endangered crocodile species in the world. It has a very small range, living only in the Zapata Swamp in the southwestern part of mainland Cuba and in the Lanier Swamp on Isla de la Juventud. The Cuban crocodile's entire habitat measures just 200 square miles (518 sq km).[10]

> About 95 percent of Cuba's frog species are endemic to the nation, meaning they are not found anywhere else in the world.[13]

A healthy Cuban crocodile can live up to 75 years, but humans pose a great risk to this species. People have long hunted the animal for its meat and hide. The crocodiles' hides are used to make leather goods such as shoes, belts, and handbags. Others kill the species because they view the animal as a threat to humans and livestock. About 3,000 Cuban crocodiles remain in the wild.[11]

At just 0.4 inches (1 cm) long, the Monte Iberia eleuth is the smallest frog in the Northern Hemisphere.[12] This species, which is smaller than a dime, is found only in the rainforest in a small part of eastern Cuba, and it is critically endangered. Like many amphibian species on the island, this tiny frog has become a victim of habitat loss due to deforestation.

A small number of Monte Iberia eleuths live in Cuba's Alexander von Humboldt National Park, which gives the species some protection. This frog also has some notable self-defense abilities. When the species senses danger, it emits a foul odor meant to keep predators away. It also produces a toxin that can paralyze the muscles of predators such as birds, fish, and toads. Still, these defenses may not be enough to save this species, which also reproduces more slowly than many other frog species.

As a top predator in the mangrove forests along Cuba's coast, Cuban crocodiles depend on this disappearing ecosystem.

CHAPTER **FOUR**

HISTORY

Indigenous people have lived in Cuba for thousands of years. The Ciboney and the Guanahatabey peoples inhabited the island as early as 4,000 BCE. The Ciboney lived on the small islands along Cuba's southern coast. Their name came from an Indigenous word meaning "cave dweller," describing where many Ciboney people lived. The Guanahatabey made their homes in the far western part of the main island in what would later become the Pinar del Río Province.

Beginning around 300 BCE, the Taíno people came to the region. Cuba's name came from the Taíno word *coabana*, which means "great place" in their language. The Ciboney and the Guanahatabey peoples were hunter-gatherers, but the Taíno farmed

The Castillo de la Real Fuerza was built between 1558 and 1577 to protect Havana from pirates. It is now a UNESCO World Heritage site.

After establishing settlements in Cuba, Diego Velázquez de Cuéllar sent expeditions to Mexico to conquer the people who lived there.

the land. The Taíno established villages and used early technology, such as pottery, in daily life. Although interactions between the groups were mostly peaceful, the Taíno took over much of the land without conflict. This group also settled in other parts of the Caribbean, such as the Bahamas. By the 1400s, about 90 percent of Cuba's population were members of the Taíno group.[1]

SPANISH COLONIZATION

In 1492, Italian explorer Christopher Columbus arrived in Cuba, claiming the land for Spain. A Spaniard named Diego Velázquez de Cuéllar was later placed in charge of taking the island from the Indigenous people. Beginning in 1511, Velázquez spent several years establishing Spanish settlements in Baracoa, Bayamo, Santiago, and Havana. In 1514, he was named

Cuba's governor. Around this time, more Spanish settlers began arriving in Cuba to begin new lives in the Caribbean.

One of the things that Spain hoped to find in Cuba was gold. While the island did indeed have some deposits of this valuable metal, the amount was far less than Spain had hoped. Instead, the Spaniards learned that Cuba's climate and soil were ideal for growing certain crops. The Spaniards established numerous plantations on the island. Soon, the colonists were exporting coffee, sugar, and tobacco to both Europe and parts of North America.

The Indigenous people suffered greatly under Spanish rule. The colonists imposed a system called *encomienda*, which required the Indigenous people to adopt Christianity. The system also forced the Indigenous people to perform hard labor in Spain's gold mines and on its plantations in exchange for their religious instruction.

The European settlers also unknowingly carried deadly illnesses, such as smallpox. The Indigenous people had not previously been exposed to these diseases, so they had not developed immunity to the illnesses. Most of the Indigenous people died within a few decades of when Columbus arrived.

INDENTURED WORKERS FROM CHINA

Between 1847 and 1874, about 140,000 Chinese people were brought to Cuba as indentured workers. Promised a life of opportunity, they were obligated to work at least eight years on the sugar plantations.[2] But these people did not realize the harsh conditions that awaited them on the other side of the world. The plantation owners were given absolute power over the Chinese workers. Owners controlled and punished the indentured workers with leg chains, beatings, and even executions.

> By 1838, there were almost 400,000 enslaved people in Cuba.[5]

When he first came to Cuba, between 50,000 and 300,000 Indigenous people lived on the island.[3] By 1550, only about 3,000 Indigenous people were left.[4]

With so few Indigenous people left to work on plantations, the Spaniards looked to another part of the world for their labor. They began enslaving thousands of people from West Africa and taking them to Cuba to work on the island's plantations. Slavery continued in Cuba for more than 300 years, creating large amounts of wealth for Spain.

WARS FOR INDEPENDENCE

By the mid-1800s, many people in Cuba were unhappy under Spanish rule. They paid high taxes and had no representation in the country's government. Fed up with unfair treatment from corrupt leaders, a group of planters in eastern Cuba thought it was time for the end of Spanish rule. Led by Carlos Manuel de Céspedes, this group declared Cuba's independence in 1868. This marked the beginning of the Ten Years' War (1868–1878).

People had different reasons for wanting independence from Spain. Many wealthy landowners wanted more money and power. Cuba was now the leading sugar producer in the world, yet it was the Spaniards who were becoming richest from these exports. Landowners often had influence in lawmaking because of their wealth. But they wanted even more control so they didn't have to pay Spain so much in taxes. Farmers with less land and fewer workers wanted to end slavery on

JOSÉ MARTÍ

One of the biggest supporters of Cuba's independence from Spain was essayist and poet José Martí. Despite being exiled to Spain twice as punishment for his involvement with revolutionary groups, he remained dedicated to Cuba's struggle for freedom from Spanish rule. In 1892, Martí became the head of the Cuban Revolutionary Party. Three years later, he died in battle at Dos Ríos. More than 130 years later, he is still known as a symbol for freedom throughout Latin America.

the island. They also wanted a voice in how the government was run.

About 200,000 people died in the war, which had no victors.[6] The Cubans were not well organized, and they didn't have the support of other nations. The United States watched the conflict play out but did not intervene. In 1878, Spain offered to make political reforms in Cuba if the Cuban people ended their fight. The Cubans agreed to stop fighting and kept pushing for the end of slavery. Spain formally abolished the practice eight years later.

Despite these changes, Spain continued to raise taxes in Cuba. By the mid-1890s, people in Cuba were on the verge of another revolt against Spain. In 1895, Spain canceled a trade agreement Cuba had made with the United States. Cuba had made the agreement without seeking Spain's approval. The relationship between Cuba and the United States had been strengthening at this time. Cuba once again pushed for independence from Spain, declaring itself the Republic of Cuba in September. Conflict between Cuba and Spain then increased with the Cuban War of Independence (1895–1898).

At first, it seemed as if Spain was going to win the war. Spain put General Valeriano Weyler y Nicolau in charge. He was a military general nicknamed *El Carnicero*, which meant "The Butcher." Living up to his reputation, he sent many Cuban people to concentration camps, in which tens of thousands died of disease or starvation.

But Cuba soon received help from an unexpected source. In February 1898, an explosion rocked the USS *Maine* in Havana Harbor, sinking the US military vessel. Although no one could prove who attacked the ship, many people in the United States blamed Spain. Two months later, the United States joined Cuba's war effort. By December, the United States had won the Spanish-American War (1898), with the Treaty of Paris officially ending the conflict. US forces remained in Cuba for more than three years, but in 1902, the Republic of Cuba finalized an agreement for US withdrawal from the new nation.

THE CUBAN REVOLUTION

In 1902, Tomás Estrada Palma became Cuba's first president. Over the next several decades, many Cuban people prospered due to the country's continued sugar exports. In time, though, government corruption became a problem once again. By the 1930s, a military sergeant named

> **THE PLATT AMENDMENT**
>
> Cuba signed a treaty with the United States in the early 1900s that gave its northern neighbor certain rights in Cuba's affairs. The Platt Amendment gave the US government permission to set up naval bases in Cuba and to intervene in any matters that threatened Cuban independence. The treaty also gave the United States the right to restrict any treaties that Cuba made with other nations.

In the late 1890s, insurrectionists gathered in the jungle to plan their next attack. Under Céspedes's direction, they fought to abolish slavery and join the United States.

By 1957, Fidel Castro, *center*, and his troop commanders were meeting regularly at a secret base in the jungle along the coast.

Fulgencio Batista began his rise to power. First elected president in 1940, he left office four years later after losing the next election. He moved to the United States for a brief period. Upon returning to Cuba in 1952, he staged a successful government takeover. The United States did not support this move, but the US government quickly acknowledged Batista as Cuba's new leader. At first, the people welcomed Batista's return, hoping he would end the corruption that still existed at the highest levels. But Batista soon became a dictator. He embezzled money from the government and used violence to stop all political opposition.

Among the many people who wanted Batista out of power was a University of Havana law school graduate named Fidel Castro. He had originally planned to run for office, but when Batista seized control of the country, Castro instead started organizing a revolutionary movement to oust the dictator. His efforts were largely unsuccessful in the beginning, but by the late 1950s, he had attracted many people to his cause.

One of Castro's biggest weapons against Batista was propaganda. He used radio broadcasts and interviews with journalists to help spread his message that Batista was a brutal and corrupt dictator. The revolutionaries also used more basic methods for reaching the people of Cuba. Images of a young Fidel Castro appeared on walls throughout Havana. Revolutionaries wrote slogans such as *Yo soy la revolución* (I am the revolution), *¡Venceremos!* (We will win!), and *Socialismo o Muerte* over advertisements on billboards throughout the nation. Meaning "socialism or death," this phrase served as a motto for Castro's revolutionary movement. It also summed up the changes Castro wanted to make to Cuba's government.

In 1959, Castro's vision became a reality when the revolutionaries forced Batista to give up power and flee Cuba for the Dominican Republic. Castro took control of the government. Although he wasn't a dictator at first, he soon became one. Under Castro's lead, Cuba was moving toward a socialist system.

THE CUBAN MISSILE CRISIS

As the first and only communist country in the Western Hemisphere, Cuba did not have a close relationship with any of its neighbors. Communism is a one-party system of government in which all resources and means of production are owned by the state. Other communist nations, such as China and North Korea, were on the other side of the world. The Soviet Union was also a powerful nation that practiced communism. Near the beginning of Castro's regime, Cuba began to align itself with the Soviet Union. This alignment caused problems in Cuba's relationship with the United States—a democracy that strongly opposed communism.

During World War II (1939–1945), the United States and the Soviet Union had worked together to defeat Germany. But as new boundaries were established in the areas of Europe and Asia that had been affected by the war, some of the countries became communist while others became democracies. The Soviet Union and the United States became increasingly more hostile to one another. They also began to compete in a race to win more countries over to their respective forms of government. Cuba became a key battleground in this fight, which became known as the Cold War (1947–1991).

One of the anti-tank missiles placed on Cuban soil in 1962 is on display at the Morro Cabaña complex. In 2012, Cuba observed the fiftieth anniversary of the crisis.

The Cold War had made the United States and the Soviet Union enemies. Although no actual battles took place between the countries, neither of them took this rivalry lightly. Each country developed advanced new weapons in an effort to make itself the more dominant superpower. In 1962, Cuba allowed the Soviet Union to place missiles that could carry nuclear weapons on the island. Through military spying, the United States soon learned of these deadly weapons, which could hit US cities if fired. This led to a confrontation known as the Cuban Missile Crisis, bringing the United States and the Soviet Union to the brink of war. The Soviet Union ultimately agreed to remove the weapons to avoid this outcome, but the relationship between Cuba and the United States remained strained.

The situation worsened when Soviet leader Nikita Khrushchev made an agreement with US president John F. Kennedy to withdraw the missiles as long as the United States agreed not to invade Cuba. In a secret deal, Kennedy promised to remove US missiles that the country had placed in Turkey starting in 1961, as Khrushchev saw that as too close to the Soviet Union.

Castro was completely unaware of the agreement until he learned about it from Carlos Franqui, a friend who was also the editor of a large newspaper. Castro was furious over the matter. He felt as if the Soviet Union had treated Cuba as an unimportant island nation.

When the Soviet Union dissolved in 1991, Cuba's trade lessened overall. This was a time of great economic hardship for the Caribbean nation. Cuba eventually started trading with Russia again in the late 1990s. The relationship between the two nations improved steadily after this time. But Cuba remained heavily isolated from the rest of the world for the nearly 49 years that Castro was in power.

TRANSITION OF POWER

As Castro got older, his health started to decline. In 2006, he began handing over control of the country to his brother Raúl, who took full control in 2008. The United States saw the transition of power as an opportunity. US president Barack Obama announced that the United States would reopen trade between the nations if Cuba began moving toward democracy. Although changes were made slowly, including some back-and-forth shifts, Cuba gradually started reopening to the rest of the world. After serving as Cuba's leader for ten years, Raúl Castro stepped down in 2018. He named Miguel Díaz-Canel as his replacement.

Economic struggles for the people of Cuba had long been issues during the Castros' rule, and these problems continued under Díaz-Canel. Power outages, food shortages, and lack of necessary medicines are challenges the people still deal with on a regular basis. Some Cuban citizens have taken part in government protests because of these issues. Cuba has responded by arresting many of the protesters and limiting the public's access to the media.

Cuban president Miguel Díaz-Canel spoke before the United Nations Climate Summit in December 2023.

CHAPTER **FIVE**

PEOPLE AND CULTURE

Nearly 11 million people live in Cuba. The total population of the country decreased by about 10 percent between 2022 and 2024, with as many as one million people leaving the nation during that time.[1] Experts blamed Cuba's worsening economy for this mass migration. Many Cubans who wanted better job and life opportunities began seeking them elsewhere.

Another factor in Cuba's decreased population was the nation's low birth rate. From the end of 2021 to the end of 2023, more than 400,000 Cubans died while about 284,000 babies were born in the nation.[2] However, Cubans have a life expectancy of 78.3 years.[3] This is much higher than the global average of 72 years.[4]

In Havana's city plazas, Cuban people and tourists gather to learn salsa dance moves.

Nearly 900 historic buildings make up Old Havana, which is centered on five plazas. The architecture is influenced by a mix of Spanish, French, British, and Caribbean styles.

More than 80 percent of Cuba's population live in urban areas, while the remaining 20 percent reside in rural regions of the country. The largest city, Havana, is home to more than 2.1 million people. The next most populous cities are Santiago de Cuba with about 555,000 people and Camagüey with about 347,000.[5]

CUBAN ARCHITECTURE

Cuba's diverse cultural heritage is represented in its variety of architectural styles. In Old Havana, people can visit historic buildings inspired by several time periods and places around the world. One of the best examples of baroque style, which originated in Italy, is found in the Cathedral of Havana. This structure, which was built in the 1700s, is known for its asymmetrical towers. One tower is both taller and wider than the other. Baroque buildings are also known for carvings and decorative high ceilings.

El Templete, a temple constructed in 1828, is an example of neoclassical architecture. This style, which originated in Europe in the 1700s, is known for minimal decoration. Although El Templete is small compared with most other structures in Old Havana, its columns and iron fencing give it a significant presence. El Templete was built on the site of the first mass and town council meeting, which was held in the city in 1519. A mass is a Catholic church service.

Built for the rum company of the same name, the Edificio Bacardí was the first example of art deco architecture in Cuba. The style is known for bold geometric patterns such as zigzags and chevrons. The 12-story structure was finished in 1930 and was also the tallest building on the island at that time.[6]

LANGUAGES

Like many of the other countries in the Caribbean, Central America, and South America, Spanish is Cuba's national language. Cuban Spanish differs in small ways from the Spanish spoken elsewhere, however. For example, some Cuban Spanish words can be traced to the language of the Taíno people. These include the word *canoa*, which means "canoe," and the word *carey*, which means "tortoiseshell."

The second most common language heard in Cuba is Haitian Creole. This language is spoken mainly by immigrants from Haiti and other people of Haitian heritage. The language is so common in Cuba that a radio station broadcasts entirely in

SAME LANGUAGE, DIFFERENT SOUNDS

Cuban Spanish differs a bit from the Spanish language spoken in Spain. Consonants have a more relaxed pronunciation in Cuba, especially at the ends of words. In Cuban Spanish, for example, when the letter *s* or the letter *d* appears at the end of a syllable, it sounds similar to the letter *h* or is silent. This pronunciation is also common in other Caribbean nations.

Haitian Creole. Other common languages among Cuba's immigrant populations include Galician, which is spoken by many people from Spain, and Corsican, which is spoken by many people from Italy. Lucumí, a language that combines Spanish with several Bantu languages from Africa, is a popular second language among people who practice Santeria. This religion originated in Cuba.

> About 28 million people in the Caribbean speak Spanish. Most of them live in Cuba, the Dominican Republic, and Puerto Rico.[7]

CUBAN FOOD

Cuban food has many influences. Elements of Spanish, African, American, Chinese, Italian, and Taíno cuisines can all be found in different Cuban dishes. Spanish cuisine is by far the most influential, however. Many of Cuba's most popular recipes have been adapted from Spanish country cooking. Picadillo is a dish made with ground meat, tomatoes, and potatoes. Churros are fried pastries dusted with sugar and cinnamon. Other popular Cuban dishes involve large amounts of beans, garlic, and pork.

With all the country's coffee plantations, coffee is also enormously popular in Cuba. While its pleasing scent is similar to the coffee prepared in the United States, the Cuban version of the drink tastes a lot different. Cuban coffee is about twice as strong as American coffee. Many people compare it to espresso. Cuban coffee is also thicker, closer to the consistency of syrup. This is in part due to a sugary paste called *espuma* that is used to sweeten the beverage. Espuma, which means "foam" in Spanish, is made by mixing sugar with espresso.

Ropa vieja, one of Cuba's traditional dishes, is often made with shredded beef and served with rice and plantains.

One of the most popular foods in this Caribbean country is the Cuban sandwich. It begins with Cuban bread, which is soft and similar to Italian bread. Inside the sandwich, there are slices of ham, roast pork, Swiss cheese, pickles, and mustard. The sandwich is grilled until the bread is golden brown and the cheese is melted. Many people like this popular sandwich because it is flavorful, affordable, and easy to find nearly anywhere in Cuba.

Another beloved part of Cuban cuisine is *mojo criollo* sauce. This sauce, which is often added to chicken, pork, or vegetables, is typically prepared using garlic, oil, and sour orange juice. The combination of flavors is inspired by both Spanish and African cultures. Meat and vegetables cooked in mojo criollo sauce are often paired with rice and beans. White rice and black beans are among the most common side dishes in Cuban cuisine.

At the end of many Cuban meals, flan is served as dessert. This caramel custard is made with milk, eggs, sugar, and vanilla. While flan dates back to the Roman Empire, Cuba is known for making some of the best flan in the world. It can be found on nearly all dessert menus in Cuban restaurants, although many Cuban people insist that the very best versions of this favorite dessert are homemade.

Known for having a large immigrant population, Cuba also has a variety of restaurants that serve food from other cultures. Hamburgers, pizza, and Chinese food are common fare throughout the country. Some Cuban restaurant owners also put their own spin on dishes from other cultures. For example, many rural restaurants are known for serving their own versions of Chinese fried rice by using local meats, vegetables, and spices.

MINI BIO

DESI ARNAZ

Desi Arnaz was a famous actor, musician, and business executive from Cuba. Born in Santiago on March 2, 1917, he was best known for the US television series *I Love Lucy*. He appeared in the popular show alongside his wife, Lucille Ball, in the 1950s. Arnaz was also the show's cocreator and producer.

Born into a wealthy family, Arnaz was the son of a Cuban politician and the grandson of one of the founders of the Bacardí rum company. At 16, Arnaz was forced to flee Cuba with his family after Fulgencio Batista took control of the government in 1933. With little money, the family had to start over in the United States.

After working several low-paying jobs, Arnaz began working as a musician. His talent for playing the drums and the guitar led him to play in Latin orchestras. He also appeared in a Broadway musical and starred in several films.

I Love Lucy was based on Arnaz's real-life marriage to Ball. His character was a fun-loving bandleader named Ricky Ricardo, who was also from Cuba.

In Old Havana, dancers perform a traditional African dance to the beat of drums.

MUSIC AND DANCE

Much like Cuba's food, its music has been significantly influenced by other cultures. Spanish and African cultures have had the biggest impact by far. Spanish colonists, enslaved people from West Africa, and Chinese immigrants all brought different musical styles to the island. By the early 1900s, Santeria had also become a musical influence, with percussion playing a large part in many religious ceremonies.

One of the most popular types of music in Cuba is called *son Cubano*, which means "the sound of Cuba." It combines sounds from the Cuban guitar with African rhythms and heavy bass. Originating in the city of Matanzas, son Cubano eventually spread to other parts of Cuba and later to other parts of the world. A dance-music version of son Cubano became especially popular in New York City's nightclubs in the 1950s.

Dance clubs playing this music are still popular in Cuba. Son Cubano inspired another popular dance style called salsa, which is also a type of music. The fast-paced movements include lots of quick foot movements and spins. Many Cuban people insist that salsa is much more than these two things, though. Some call it an emotion because of the passion that people feel when they take part in it. Also originating in African culture, rumba music and dance is especially popular in Cuba. Rumba includes both slow and quick steps. Its expressive moves are said to tell a story.

SPORTS

Baseball started making its way into the hearts of the Cuban people when the sport was introduced to the nation in 1864. A group of students who had visited the United States explained the game to

HISTORIC GOLD
After baseball was made an Olympic sport in 1992, Cuba won the first two gold medals awarded in the sport. The nation took home its first gold medal for baseball in the 1992 Olympics in Barcelona, Spain, and its second in the 1996 Olympics in Atlanta, Georgia. Although the sport has long been popular in Cuba, other nations were less interested in it. Baseball was removed from the Olympics in 2008. But baseball will be included in the 2028 Olympics in Los Angeles.

Young people in Cuba gather for neighborhood pickup games of baseball after school.

their families and friends after returning home. When the first official game was played in Cuba at Estadio Palmar de Junco in Matanzas in 1874, the sport's popularity began to soar. The stadium where that first game was played is still in operation. Of all the active baseball stadiums in the world, this one is the oldest.

The top competitive baseball league in Cuba is called the National Series, which includes 16 teams. This league was created in 1961 when Fidel Castro ended professional sports in the country as part of his new socialist regime. Castro believed that amateur sports offered an opportunity for athletes to play for the love of the game, rather than to play for money. Although top players may be paid by the government for their participation, the amounts are typically low, about $100 per month.[8] For this reason, many players have defected, or left the country, to play professional baseball in the United States.

Amateur or not, Cuban baseball games usually draw large audiences of enthusiastic fans. The games are not as well planned or organized as the ones played in many other countries, but the spectators don't let this fact stop them from

DOMINOES EVERYWHERE

The game of dominoes is incredibly popular in Cuba. To make it even more fun, the Cuban people have added their own slang to the game. They use nicknames for numbers. The number two is known as Duque Hernández, the famous baseball pitcher. While Hernández has no connection to this number, other nicknames do have a link. The number seven, for example, is known as *la peste*, a Spanish word meaning "the plague," because seven is considered unlucky in dominoes.

enjoying themselves. Similar to US baseball fans, they often watch a game while eating food from local vendors. This fare might include hamburgers, yucca chips, and soft drinks. A yucca is a potato-like vegetable that grows in Cuba.

In addition to baseball, the Cuban people enjoy a variety of other sports. These include soccer. In 2012, Cuba's soccer team won the Caribbean Cup. Cubans are also big fans of boxing. The nation has won numerous medals in international boxing competitions, including 41 Olympic golds.[9]

> In 2016, more than 55,000 baseball fans gathered at Estadio Latinoamericano in Havana to watch an exhibition game between the Tampa Bay Rays and the Cuban national team.[11]

RELIGIONS

Nearly 60 percent of the Cuban people are Christians, with most of them practicing Catholicism. Another 18 percent practice folk religions, including Santeria, a religion created by Africans in Cuba. A variety of other religions are each followed by less than 1 percent of the population in the country.[10]

Spain brought Catholicism to Cuba when it colonized the island. The religion remained popular until the Castro regime took over in the early 1960s. When the Catholic Church showed disapproval of communism, the Cuban government declared itself atheist. It banned anyone who continued to practice any faith from joining the Communist Party. The government's position on religion softened in the early 1990s when Pope John Paul II made a historic visit to the island to discuss human rights and religious freedom. In a symbolic gesture, Fidel Castro met the religious leader when he exited his plane. Although nothing was official, the fact that Castro welcomed the head of the Catholic Church made it more acceptable for other Cubans to embrace both the pope and his religion once again.

Santeria is commonly practiced throughout Cuba. This religion, which combines elements of Catholicism and Western African religions, began on the island among enslaved people. When enslaved people were forced to attend Catholic mass, they continued to worship their own gods, aligning each one with a different Catholic saint. Although the Catholic Church leaders did not realize what was happening, a new religion was coming into existence. While the Catholic Church does not officially accept Santeria, it remains popular with many Cuban people.

HOLIDAYS AND OTHER CELEBRATIONS IN CUBA

Holidays in Cuba begin with New Year's celebrations on January 1. One Cuban tradition involves the superstition of throwing a bucket of water out of the house. Its purpose is to cleanse the home of the previous year's challenges.

In July, the Cuban people celebrate the Carnival of Santiago de Cuba, which is similar to Carnival celebrations in other Latin American countries during spring. This festival features a blend of Spanish, African, and Caribbean cultures. It is celebrated with lively parades, which have elaborate floats, bands playing music, performers in colorful costumes, and dancing, including a conga line.

After Pope John Paul II visited Cuba, other popes followed, including Pope Francis in 2015.

Carnival celebrations have been held in the streets of Santiago de Cuba since the 1600s as a way to honor Cuban culture and history.

Among the most popular holidays in Cuba is Independence Day. Celebrated each year on October 10, it marks the end of Spanish rule. Cubans spend this historic anniversary watching parades, attending concerts, and going to see fireworks.

With so many Christians in Cuba, Christmas is also a popular holiday in the nation. Unlike many other countries, however, Cuba plans most of its celebrations for Christmas Eve instead of Christmas Day. Called Nochebuena, Christmas Eve typically includes large family gatherings and festive meals such as roasted pork or *tostones*. This is the Cuban name for fried plantains, which are similar to bananas.

Santa Claus is called Papá Noel in Cuba, but he is not as popular in Cuba as in many other nations. Instead of hanging a stocking for gifts on Christmas Eve, many Cuban children leave an empty shoe by the door on the eve of Día de los Reyes Magos, or Three Kings' Day, on January 6. Kids also leave a letter for their favorite king, or wise man. They ask him to place a gift in the shoe. This date is also known as the Epiphany in Catholicism.

CHAPTER SIX

POLITICS

Cuba's government is a one-party socialist republic. The nation is among the last in the world to use this system, which does not allow any rival political parties. The Cuban Communist Party holds all the political power in Cuba. Communism has undeniable influence in the country, but it is not technically the official system of government. Still, many political experts consider the nation a communist country.

Under Cuba's socialist system, the government owns and controls virtually all the major businesses and resources in the country. Only a small number of low-level private businesses are allowed to operate in Cuba. For example, some people grow herbs to sell to restaurants, while others use their automobiles for hire to drive people where they need to go. These small

It took 5,000 workers to build El Capitolio, Cuba's capitol building. Construction began in 1926 and was completed in 1929.

The Cuban government invests more than 14 percent of its annual budget in education.

business owners are called *cuentapropistas*, which means "self-employed." In communist countries, no private businesses are allowed. Cuba distributes most of the nation's wealth among its citizens according to how long, hard, or well the people work. Some Cuban citizens are allowed to become landowners. Communism distributes wealth based on need. Under this system, the government owns all property except for the smallest personal items.

The Cuban government also controls the educational system and the media. Schools and news outlets censor information, limiting it to content that promotes the socialist system. This means reading materials that question or criticize the system are hard for the average Cuban citizen to find. Although the internet is available to the people, it is also heavily censored. The government is the only internet service provider, and any content it opposes is blocked.

LIMITED FREEDOM OF THE PRESS

The Cuban Constitution states that "the people's freedom of the press is recognized." But the country prevents free presses from operating. Private ownership of mass media, such as television stations or newspapers, is not allowed in Cuba. All mass media is owned by the government. When writers such as independent journalists or bloggers are critical of the government in their articles or posts, Cuban authorities prevent the writers from sharing their work with the people.

Although education at all levels is free in Cuba, students are limited in what they can learn and how they can use their degrees. For example, students who do not show the desired amount of enthusiasm for socialism are not allowed to study the social sciences. Teachers are also restricted in which perspectives they can share in the classroom, further limiting what students can learn.

MINI BIO

MIGUEL DÍAZ-CANEL

In 2018, Miguel Díaz-Canel became the first president since the Cuban Revolution who was not from the Castro family. Díaz-Canel was born in Cuba on April 20, 1960, about a year after the revolution. As a young man, he studied to become an electrical engineer and later taught engineering at Central University of Las Villas, the school from which he graduated in 1982.

When he was a teacher, Díaz-Canel became active in the Communist Party of Cuba and became the Minister of Higher Education in 2009. After being elected first vice president in 2013, Díaz-Canel began to represent Cuba abroad. He attended the funeral of Venezuela's president Hugo Chávez in 2013. Díaz-Canel also met with world leaders such as Russia's Vladimir Putin.

When Raúl Castro stepped down as president in 2018, he chose Díaz-Canel as his successor. Díaz-Canel also became the leader of the Communist Party when Castro officially retired from politics in 2021. Although Díaz-Canel continued many of Castro's policies, he also brought a new generation's view to the presidency. He allowed more small businesses to operate and opened censored internet use to most of Cuba.

Miguel Díaz-Canel made his first overseas visit as president to Venezuela in June 2018 to show support for the newly elected president Nicolás Maduro.

SPEAKING THEIR MINDS

Young people in Cuba are often more outspoken about their political beliefs than people from older generations. Parents often worry about what will happen to their kids if they become too vocal. People as young as 15 have been detained in Cuba for expressing anti-government opinions in public or online. Still, many young people feel strongly that nothing will change if they do not speak up.

THE STRUCTURE OF CUBA'S GOVERNMENT

Cuba's government has three branches. The executive branch is run by a group of officials called the Council of Ministers. This group includes the president, the first vice president, the prime minister, the Council of State's seven vice presidents, the executive committee secretary, and a variety of other appointed and elected officials. The first vice president and the prime minister both report to the president, who holds the majority of the power. The Council of Ministers is responsible for the national budget, trade with other countries, and foreign policies.

The National Assembly of People's Power is the legislative branch. The primary job of this branch is turning the decisions made by the government's executive branch into law. The assembly is divided into departments that oversee specific parts of the government, such as local assemblies and judicial affairs. The legislative branch of Cuba's government is a unicameral parliamentary system, which means it has a single chamber.

The judicial branch of Cuba's government consists of the People's Supreme Court. As the highest court in the nation, it hears cases involving the country's constitution as well as appeals

> The National Assembly of People's Power has 470 members. This number is down from 614 members after a law was passed in 2019 to limit the number of seats.[1]

from lower-level courts. These cases may involve civil or criminal matters, labor disputes, or matters relating to the economy.

Cuba describes itself as a democratic state. In this type of government, the people hold most of the power. However, many other nations consider Cuba an authoritarian state, which places most power in the hands of a small group of leaders. Cuban law requires that all citizens 16 years or older vote in elections held every five years, but the elections are neither free nor competitive. With only one party, the people have no choice in how the government is run. Most political candidates run for office unopposed.

Women have had the right to vote in Cuba since 1934. They now also hold major roles in the government. Although men outnumber women in the National Assembly, many women serve as members. Men still occupy most government positions at the highest levels.

POLITICAL SYMBOLS

As a supporter of independence from Spain, poet and journalist Miguel Teurbe Tolón designed Cuba's flag with this goal in mind. His wife, Emilia Teurbe Tolón, sewed the first version of the flag in 1850. The design was recognized as Cuba's official flag in 1869.

Its colorful pattern has several meanings. The three blue stripes that run horizontally across the flag's background represent Cuba's three military districts. The two white stripes between the blue ones stand for the purity of the patriot cause. The red triangle on the flag's left side is a symbol of strength, and the single white star within the triangle stands for independence.

General Narciso López carried the flag in some of the earliest battles in the fight for independence. He pushed for the design to become the official flag of Cuba, which happened when Cuba became an independent nation in 1902. The design has remained the same since that time despite the numerous periods of turmoil the nation has endured.

At many events in which Cuba's flag is raised, the country's national anthem is also played. Cuba's national anthem was written by another beloved freedom fighter, Pedro Figueredo. A poet and a musician, Figueredo composed the music for "La Bayamesa" in 1867, and he wrote the words in 1868. The song became Cuba's official anthem in 1902.

The Cuban flag is displayed on many public buildings throughout the country, including the Museo de la Revolución, or Museum of the Revolution, in Havana.

Cuba takes its national symbols very seriously. A law passed in 2019 limits the use of the flag to events the government has approved. If government inspectors decide that a cultural event featuring the flag violates the law, they may shut down the event. Another law passed in 2022 states that insulting national symbols such as the flag or the national anthem can be punished with a large fine, two to five years in prison, or a combination of both. The previous punishment ranged from a smaller fine to between three months and a year in prison.

CUBA'S MILITARY

Cuba requires that all male citizens between the ages of 17 and 28 serve at least two years in the nation's military, which is called the Revolutionary Armed Forces. After this period, the men remain part of a reserve group, which means they can be called to active duty if needed until they reach the age of 45. In Cuba, boys as young as 12 years old begin early military training.

Starting in the mid-1970s, the Soviet Union began supplying Cuba with equipment to help the nation strengthen its military. By 1990, Cuba's air force had about 150 Russian fighter planes, including MiG-23 Floggers and the advanced MiG-29 Fulcrums.[2] Since the fall of the Soviet Union, however, the flow of new equipment has slowed. Cuba's military equipment has been likened to its classic cars, which have been maintained in surprising ways. For example, the Cuban Navy has turned fishing trawlers into warships by adding weapons and helicopter landing decks.

> **The Revolutionary Armed Forces has about 60,000 soldiers.**[3]

CUBA AND RUSSIA

Cuba has long had a strong relationship with Russia, and it appears to be growing even stronger. Russia supplies Cuba with many essential goods, such as steel, oil, and wheat. In return, Cuba has agreed to let Russian companies use Cuban land for the next several decades. Cuba has even agreed to waive import taxes on Russian goods. Russia hopes to make Cuba a popular destination for Russians who are interested in taking tropical vacations.

During the 1970s and 1980s, Cuba sent thousands of its soldiers to assist in insurgencies in other parts of the world, including Angola, Ethiopia, and Nicaragua. But in 1992, Castro declared that these kinds of deployments were ending. For several decades it seemed as if this practice was in the past, but Miguel Díaz-Canel sent hundreds of soldiers to Russia to help with its invasion of Ukraine beginning in 2022.

CHAPTER **SEVEN**

ECONOMICS

One of Cuba's most significant natural resources is its soil, which is ideal for growing many types of crops. Sugar and coffee are among the country's most plentiful agricultural products. Cuba is also known for growing rice, avocados, citrus fruits, bananas, plantains, corn, potatoes, and tomatoes. Some crops can yield up to two harvests each year under the right conditions.

Even with the country's rich soil, however, Cuba's crops are highly dependent on getting enough rain. In years when precipitation falls short of what farmers need, the harvests are far less plentiful. This has hurt Cuba's economy.

Because of Cuba's vast coastline, fishing has long been a big part of its economy. Hake, tilapia, tuna, lobsters, and shrimp are all found in the island's

The government distributes food grown on the island through grocery stores, or bodegas, but family rations are seldom enough to live on.

coastal waters. However, the numbers of many fish species, including groupers and snappers, have dropped in recent decades. Experts blame overfishing for this problem.

NATURAL RESOURCES AND MANUFACTURING

Cuba's most abundant mined metal is nickel, and it is among the world's top ten producers. Nickel is used for making coins, rechargeable batteries, plumbing fixtures, and other objects. It is also a popular alloy. This means it is added to other metals to make them more durable.

> **SUGAR EXPORTS DOWN**
>
> Cuba was once one of the top sugar producers in the world. In the 1980s, the Caribbean nation regularly produced 7.7 million short tons (7 million metric tons) of this food staple annually. But the country has been exporting much less sugar recently due to poor harvests and sanctions. In 2022, Cuba produced just 529,109 short tons (480,000 metric tons) of sugar. It produced even less in 2023, making it the first year Cuba exported less sugar than the nation consumed itself.[2]

Often found alongside nickel, cobalt is another abundant element in Cuba. This material is used for making lithium-ion batteries. Electric cars depend heavily on these power sources. Cobalt is also used to make aircraft engines.

Off Cuba's northern coast are oil and natural gas reserves, which are important energy sources for the nation. Cuba produces about 305 million gallons (1.2 billion L) of natural gas each year. The country's three oil fields produce about 80,000 barrels of oil each day, but this amount is still far less than Cuba needs for its electricity production, industry, and transportation.[1] The country has allowed oil companies from other nations, such as Brazil and India, to explore its oil reserves in hopes of discovering more of this in-demand fuel.

> Cuba produces about 50,000 short tons (45,000 metric tons) of nickel each year.[4]

After Cuba adopted its socialist system, trade lessened significantly between Cuba and many other nations, including the United States. The United States banned all trade between itself and Cuba with an embargo in 1962. As this happened, Cuba began trading more with other socialist countries, including the Soviet Union, East Germany, and China. By the end of the 1980s, nearly three-quarters of Cuba's trade was being conducted with the Soviet Union.[3]

Although Cuba's economy still struggles in many ways, it has thrived in the development of new pharmaceuticals, or medicines. The nation's pharmaceutical industry is one of its most successful. In 2005, Cuba developed the first synthetic vaccine against a bacterial form of influenza called Hib. This illness is particularly dangerous for children under five years of age. More recently, Cuba developed a vaccine against lung cancer. In 2016, it became the first vaccine from Cuba that the United States agreed to test for use in US patients.

CUBA'S CURRENCY

The Cuban peso became Cuba's official currency in 1881. At this time, it was the equivalent of one US dollar. Cuban coins were first minted in 1915, with a similar appearance to US coins. This was largely because they were produced in the United States. Starting in 1899, Cuba also began

In October 2024, one US dollar was equal to 24 Cuban pesos.

A CASH SHORTAGE

Cuban people often rely on cash for buying everyday goods, but a cash shortage in 2024 led people to form lines at banks. Many citizens were frustrated when they could not access cash to buy necessary items such as food and fuel. The government saw this problem coming. A year earlier, it began promoting the concept of a cashless society in which people would be able to use only credit cards for purchasing basic goods. But many Cuban businesses refused to transition to this system due to the costs for them.

accepting the US dollar as legal tender, a practice that lasted until 1951 when political tensions between the nations increased. In 1961, Cuba also stopped using the United States to produce its coins. Cuba's coins are now manufactured at the Royal Canadian Mint in Canada.

For many years, Cuba used two currencies: the Cuban peso (CUP) and the Cuban convertible peso (CUC). The CUC was introduced in 1994 to replace the US dollar in tourism transactions. The CUP was still used for domestic transactions, but because the CUC had a higher value, many people who were paid in CUP could not afford the same luxuries as people working in tourism who had access to the convertible peso.

At the end of 2020, President Miguel Díaz-Canel announced that Cuba would end its two-currency system. Starting in 2021, the CUC would no longer be acceptable currency in Cuba. Many people hoped this move would create more equality among Cuban citizens.

Cuba's worsening economy led the CUP to drop significantly in value in 2023. At one point, it took 230 Cuban pesos to equal one US dollar.[5] This was half the value of the CUP a year earlier. Rising prices made it even harder for Cubans to pay for all the things they needed.

CUBA'S INFRASTRUCTURE AND TRANSPORTATION

People who visit Cuba often say that the country appears to have stopped in time. The historic architecture and the antique cars offer a sense that everything in the nation remains as it was many years earlier. But time has indeed moved on. Many buildings and roadways in Cuba need repairs, which can be challenging due to Cuba's limited access to supplies.

Dozens of historic buildings in Old Havana were restored when UNESCO made the city a World Heritage site in 1982, but many more structures are now in disrepair. Highways and bridges are in poor condition. Since the gradual reopening of the nation, the Cuban government has realized the importance of repairing and restoring the country's infrastructure for the benefit of its own people and for the tourism industry.

In 2023, the country's aging infrastructure led to massive water shortages in Havana. Between 100,000 and 200,000 of the city's population were affected.[6] Some of them were left without running water for days due to broken motors at pump stations and other problems. Water was even more scarce in rural areas of the country,

Cuba has 6,647 miles (10,697 km) of paved roads, but many are deteriorating and signage is poor, making travel slow and treacherous.

Colonial architectural features, such as arches and wrought iron balconies, have been preserved throughout the Old Havana UNESCO site.

ON TWO WHEELS

Cuba is very bicycle friendly. Many people travel by this simple mode of transportation because owning a car is costly and parts are hard to find. Most roads, including highways, have a three-foot (1 m) bike lane.[7] Repair stalls called *poncheras* are commonly found on the side of the road. They help with bike repairs such as filling low tires or fixing flats. As with cars, spare parts for bikes can be hard to come by, but many Cubans have learned how to create makeshift parts from materials they have on hand.

where such shortages are common. Many Cuban citizens living in these areas must rely on rivers, shallow wells, or deliveries from tanker trucks for their water.

Power outages are another common problem in Cuba. Although the country is working on improving its public electricity and water systems, the demand is often far greater than what the nation can provide. The government asks that citizens conserve energy and other resources as much as possible, which makes some daily tasks such as cooking difficult.

Many travel websites say that the easiest way for tourists to get around in Cuba is by walking. Many of the attractions in Old Havana are within walking distance of one another, and there are no hills. People who need to travel farther often rely on buses or taxis. Local people often do better with the bus system, while many tourists prefer hired cars. Buses are usually crowded and rarely run on time. Many of the antique cars for which Cuba is known are used as taxis.

CHAPTER **EIGHT**

CUBA TODAY

Everyday life in Cuba is simple in many ways. The Cuban people are creative and resourceful. They know how to make do with what they have. Multiple generations often live under the same roof in the nation. It isn't unusual for a family of nine to live in a three-bedroom home. Sharing resources is second nature to the Cuban people.

Although the Cuban people now have access to the internet, it is expensive and slow, and the service is unreliable. Connecting to wireless internet networks in public places costs money in Cuba. And users cannot connect to many websites, including many social media sites, because of sanctions from other nations.

Family members from older generations often tell younger family members that they should appreciate the way things are now. But many young Cubans

In Cuba's smaller towns, daily life has a slower pace. Families take time to visit or play dominoes together.

hadn't been born when Fidel Castro ruled the country, so their understanding of what life was like then is limited. Today there is greater access to technology, and private businesses have become more common.

Many young people feel it is wrong that they cannot travel freely to other countries. When a family member in another nation gets married, has a baby, or is ill, it is nearly impossible for relatives in Cuba to get permission from the government to travel to see them. International travel is permitted by law in Cuba for family visits, education, and medical care. However, many average Cuban citizens often can't afford travel costs.

EDUCATION

Children in Cuba enter the first grade when they are six years old. They remain in primary school until they have completed the sixth grade. During the lower primary grades, kids learn about a variety of subjects including health and hygiene, reading and writing, and Cuba's revolutionary history. In the higher primary grades, students learn about

SUPPORTING THE CUBAN PEOPLE

One of the biggest misconceptions that Americans have about Cuba is that the country is closed off to people from the United States. Many Americans can purchase a plane ticket to Cuba by choosing one of twelve reasons for the visit. In 2023, more than 130,000 Americans visited Cuba.[1] While tourism is not listed as an option, there is an option labeled "Support the Cuban people." This is the most commonly selected reason for visiting Cuba, as most tourist activities fall into the category of supporting the Cuban people. They might include taking tours, eating at restaurants, or shopping, all of which support the Cuban economy.

> ## THE UNIVERSITY OF HAVANA
>
> Founded in 1728, the University of Havana is the oldest, largest, and most respected university in the nation. About 6,000 students enroll at the University of Havana each year.[2] As many as 25 specialties are taught at the school in such fields as Afro-Caribbean studies, music, literature, philosophy, sociology, history, biology, and international relations. The school also conducts research in economics, sciences, social science, and the humanities. But the government places restrictions on what instructors can teach. For example, professors are not allowed to teach topics that are considered anti-revolutionary.

subjects such as natural science, geography, and economics. Physical education is required throughout primary school.

Middle school in Cuba includes grades seven, eight, and nine. During these years, students start studying more advanced subjects such as languages, technology, and social sciences. At the end of middle school, students move on to either secondary school or a vocational school that teaches trade skills such as automotive repair. These schools are similar to high schools in the United States. Students attending secondary school in Cuba must meet high academic standards and spend their vacations performing some type of community service.

Vocational schools offer two paths. Some students study trades such as masonry or plumbing, preparing to enter related careers upon graduation. Other students go through programs that teach them to become middle-level technicians to perform jobs such as electronics repair work. They may then go on to technology institutes to train for their future careers, such as household appliance repair.

> **Cuba has a literacy rate of 99.67 percent among people age 15 years and older.[3]**

Many secondary school graduates go on to become university students. Once they have graduated, they must then devote the same number of years they spent attending college to working in parts of Cuba where they are most needed. They are paid for this work but at lower-than-average salaries for their professions.

WHAT KIDS IN CUBA DO FOR FUN

Kids in Cuba spend much of their free time outdoors. Children playing baseball or soccer are a common sight in many city streets. Kids living in rural areas spend much of their time playing outside as well. Unlike young people in many other countries, kids in Cuba rarely stay indoors playing video games or surfing social media. This is largely because they have limited access to electronic gadgets. Getting outside regularly to be physically active is a habit that most Cuban children develop at a young age.

Young people in Cuba also spend some of their time outdoors gardening. After the Soviet Union collapsed in the 1990s, Cuba needed new sources for food. Many cities started urban gardening programs to help fill this need. People living in cities started growing vegetables in raised beds in vacant lots, on rooftops, and even in small patches of land between buildings. The focus was on using every available resource to grow food. The practice continues in modern times. Gardening is also common among those who live in Cuba's rural areas.

After school, many Cuban kids gather to play soccer in the streets of small towns.

Cubans took to the streets in July 2021 to protest shortages of food and medicine, electricity blackouts, and the government's restrictive rules during the COVID-19 pandemic.

MEDICAL CARE SHORTAGES

Although health care is free to all Cuba's citizens, the country is experiencing a major health-care crisis. Due to trade restrictions from the United States and other nations, the Cuban government has a hard time importing many medicines and the materials needed to manufacture medicines inside the country. This means medicines and other supplies that health-care workers need to treat patients are in short supply as well.

CUBAN RESOURCEFULNESS

Food, bottled water, and fuel are just a few of the necessities that are sometimes in short supply in Cuba. Many people deal with these shortages by being resourceful. They call this *inventar*, which means "to make something out of thin air" in English. When fixing a car, for example, a Cuban mechanic may need to build a new part from pieces of broken items.

Doctors have also become a limited resource in Cuba. According to the National Statistics and Information Office, as many as 12,000 doctors left the Cuban public health system in 2022.[4] When Cuban people become ill, they often must wait months or even years for treatment, if they get treated at all. Some people try to buy medicines on their own, but the country's struggling economy makes many products hard to find and expensive when they can be tracked down.

Demand for medical care is often especially high in rural areas of Cuba, where clinics have even fewer resources. Some of these clinics ask patients to bring their own food and bedding for their stays. There are health-care facilities that are forced to reuse certain supplies, including syringes, which are needed to give vaccines and shots. Without access to new sterile supplies, these clinics aren't able to provide safe and effective treatment. Many clinics also have aging equipment, such as outdated X-ray machines, and lack supplies such as the film this old technology needs to operate.

LIMITED FREEDOM OF EXPRESSION

Cuban citizens sometimes grow impatient with their lack of resources or the government's restrictions on their personal freedoms. In 2021, a combination of the economic crisis and the

COVID-19 pandemic pushed the Cuban people to speak out. Many citizens gathered in the streets to protest these and other problems in the nation several times that year. The government responded by arresting more than 1,500 peaceful protesters and keeping hundreds of them in prison until the following year.[5] The prisoners were not allowed to make phone calls or receive visits from family members or lawyers. Some of the prisoners were also beaten or denied sleep. Many people and organizations that advocate for human rights consider the way the protesters were treated to be a violation of human rights.

When protesters appeared before a court of law, the trials often happened behind closed doors where the public could not witness them. A performance artist named Luis Manuel Otero Alcántara was punished for simply planning to join one of the 2021 protests. He was arrested shortly after posting an online video in which he shared that he was going to take part in a protest in his hometown of Havana. After being held for months in a maximum-security prison, he was sentenced to five years for his crime of planning to protest.[6]

The Cuban government defends the country's regime. Cuba has refused to allow international rights organizations such as Amnesty International into the country. Amnesty International has responded by issuing repeated invitations to Cuban president Miguel Díaz-Canel to discuss the situation and make human rights a bigger priority in the nation.

Experts do not expect Cuba's government to become a democracy, despite the demands of many of its citizens. The government continues to limit people's personal freedoms. For this reason, it is unlikely that nations will remove sanctions. This has a negative effect on the economy.

On the weekends, the streets of many Cuban cities are often filled with musicians who play rumba or salsa tunes for money.

Despite its considerable challenges, Cuba has a culture as vibrant as its turquoise ocean water. Tourists delight in the country's delicious food, lively music and dance, and array of architectural styles. But it is the Cuban people's traditions, warmth, and resilience that form the strong culture of this Caribbean nation.

ESSENTIAL FACTS

OFFICIAL NAME: REPUBLIC OF CUBA

GEOGRAPHY

Area: 42,803 square miles (110,860 sq km)

Highest Elevation: Pico Turquino at 6,476 feet (1,974 m)

Lowest Elevation: Caribbean Sea at 0 feet (0 m)

PEOPLE

Population: 10.97 million (2024 est.)

Most Populous City: Havana (2.149 million)

Ethnic Groups: White, mixed, Black

Religions: Christianity, folk religions, Buddhism, Hinduism, Judaism, Islam, other, none

GOVERNMENT

Type of Government: Socialist republic

Capital: Havana

Head of State: President

Head of Government: Prime minister

Legislature: Unicameral, with the National Assembly of People's Power

ECONOMY

Currency: Cuban peso

Major Industries: Mining, agriculture, industrial production, petroleum extraction and refining, pharmaceutical production, construction

Natural Resources: Cobalt, nickel, iron ore, chromium, copper, salt, timber, silica, petroleum, farmable land

NATIONAL SYMBOLS

National Anthem: "La Bayamesa" ("The Bayamo Song")

National Bird: Cuban trogon

National Flower: White mariposa

GLOSSARY

abolitionist
A person who wants to end slavery.

archipelago
A group of islands, or a stretch of sea containing many islands.

atheist
Not believing in the existence of any god.

authoritarian
Describing a political system that concentrates power in the hands of a leader or small ruling elite and limits civil and political freedoms and rights.

embezzle
To take illegally for one's own use.

immunity
The ability to be exposed to an illness without catching it.

infrastructure
The physical structures, such as roads, railways, and power plants, that make it possible for a city or nation to function.

insurgency
A revolt against the government.

intertidal zone
The area between high and low tide where the ocean and land meet.

propaganda
The deliberate spreading of ideas to influence people.

resilience
The ability to thrive despite great challenge.

sanction
An action taken to punish a country or force it to follow international laws.

sediment
Tiny pieces of sand, rock, and other material that are carried by water and settle at the bottom of a body of water.

socialist
Supporting an economic system in which the government controls the economy.

ADDITIONAL RESOURCES

SELECTED BIBLIOGRAPHY

Alonso, Nathalie. "The Rich History of Baseball in Cuba." *Major League Baseball*, 24 Feb. 2023, mlb.com. Accessed 18 Oct. 2024.

Clouse, Carey. "Cuba's Urban Farming Revolution." *Architectural Review*, 17 Mar. 2014, architectural-review.com. Accessed 18 Oct. 2024.

"Cuba Wildlife Facts." *PBS*, 1 Apr. 2020. pbs.org. Accessed 18 Oct. 2024.

FURTHER READINGS

Hudak, Heather C. *Focus on Cuba*. Crabtree, 2024.

Jaskulka, Marie. *United States*. Abdo, 2026.

Sheppard, Charles. *Coral Reefs: A Natural History*. Princeton University, 2021.

ONLINE RESOURCES

To learn more about Cuba, please visit **abdobooklinks.com** or scan this QR code. These links are routinely monitored and updated to provide the most current information available.

MORE INFORMATION

For more information on this subject, contact or visit the following organizations:

Havana Times

havanatimes.org

The *Havana Times* is an independent website that aims to provide a balanced view of events, policies, the government, and foreign policy in Cuba. The site also provides news on Nicaragua and Chile.

UNESCO World Heritage Convention

World Heritage Centre
7 place de Fontenoy
75352 Paris 07 SP
France
whc.unesco.org

The United Nations Educational, Scientific and Cultural Organization (UNESCO) works to identify and protect sites around the world that are believed to be of outstanding value to humanity. This site provides a history of the organization and information on the World Heritage sites.

SOURCE NOTES

CHAPTER 1. A TOUR OF CUBA
1. "Jose Marti International Airport—HAV." *Cuba Airports*, n.d., airportcuba.net. Accessed 6 Dec. 2024.
2. "Cuba Serves as Home to Thousands of Classic American Cars." *7 News WSVN*, 27 Dec. 2015, wsvn.com. Accessed 6 Dec. 2024.
3. "Cuba Population." *Worldometer*, 1 July 2023, worldometers.info. Accessed 6 Dec. 2024.

CHAPTER 2. GEOGRAPHY
1. Franklin W. Knight and Sandra H. Levinson. "Cuba." *Britannica*, 5 Dec. 2024, britannica.com. Accessed 6 Dec. 2024.
2. "Cuba Wildlife Facts." *PBS*, 1 Apr. 2020, pbs.org. Accessed 6 Dec. 2024.
3. "Cuba." *CIA World Factbook*, 24 Nov. 2024, cia.gov. Accessed 6 Dec. 2024.
4. "Isla de la Juventud." *Britannica*, 6 Nov. 2024, britannica.com. Accessed 6 Dec. 2024.
5. "Fun Facts & Trivia." *RI.gov*, n.d., ri.gov. Accessed 6 Dec. 2024.
6. Jan Schipper. "Cuban Dry Forests." *One Earth*, 23 Sept. 2020, oneearth.org. Accessed 6 Dec. 2024.
7. Jan Schipper. "Cuban Moist Forests." *One Earth*, 23 Sept. 2020, oneearth.org. Accessed 6 Dec. 2024.
8. James Wreford Watson and Paul F. Hoffman. "North America." *Britannica*, 3 Dec. 2024, britannica.com. Accessed 6 Dec. 2024.
9. "La Gran Piedra." *Beyond the Ordinary*, 18 June 2020, beyondtheordinary.co.uk. Accessed 6 Dec. 2024.
10. "La Gran Piedra." *Lonely Planet*, 2024, lonelyplanet.com. Accessed 6 Dec. 2024.
11. "Escambray Mountains." *Beyond the Ordinary*, 4 Dec. 2020, beyondtheordinary.co.uk. Accessed 6 Dec. 2024.
12. Knight and Levinson, "Cuba."
13. "Cauto River." *Britannica*, 3 Dec. 2024, britannica.com. Accessed 6 Dec. 2024.
14. Maria Alejandra Perez. "Volumes, Caves, Bodies, Relatedness: The Case of Cuban Speleology and National Defense." *Science Direct*, Dec. 2021, sciencedirect.com. Accessed 6 Dec. 2024.
15. "Río Toa, Cuba." *Trip Cuba*, n.d., tripcuba.org. Accessed 6 Dec. 2024.
16. Amanda Bedia. "The Fascinating Yumurí River Canyon." *Cuba Plus*, 12 Sept. 2023, cubaplusmagazine.com. Accessed 6 Dec. 2024.
17. "Major Rivers of the Island of Cuba." *World Atlas*, 2024, worldatlas.com. Accessed 6 Dec. 2024.
18. "Climate in Cuba." *Climates to Travel*, n.d., climatestotravel.com. Accessed 6 Dec. 2024.
19. "Cuba—Cayman Islands." *Freshwater Ecoregions of the World*, 2019, feow.org. Accessed 6 Dec. 2024.
20. "Cuba." *Climate Change Knowledge Portal*, 2021, climateknowledgeportal.worldbank.org. Accessed 6 Dec. 2024.
21. Andrea Rodriguez and Desmond Boylan. "20-Foot Waves, Persistent Storm Surge Swamp Havana in Irma's Wake." *Columbus Dispatch*, 10 Sept. 2017, dispatch.com. Accessed 14 Jan. 2025.
22. "Hurricane Ian, Cuba." *Humanitarian Coalition*, Sept. 2022, humanitariancoalition.ca. Accessed 6 Dec. 2024.
23. "Irma Hits Cuba with 160 mph Winds." *Financial Times*, 9 Sept. 2017, ft.com. Accessed 6 Dec. 2024.

CHAPTER 3. PLANTS AND ANIMALS

1. "Take a Walk on Cuba's Green Side." *Cuba Unbound*, 2024, cubaunbound.com. Accessed 6 Dec. 2024.
2. Alina Veranes. "The Fine and Wonderful Cuban Orchids." *CubaPlus*, 25 Jan. 2023. cubaplusmagazine.com. Accessed 14 Jan. 2025.
3. "Take a Walk on Cuba's Green Side."
4. Rufina Kaloyanova. "Cuba's Endangered Species." *Love Cuba*, 9 Jan. 2023, lovecuba.com. Accessed 6 Dec. 2024.
5. "Rare and Beautiful Birds of Cuba." *CubaExplorer*, 2024, cubaexplorer.com. Accessed 6 Dec. 2024.
6. "Cuban Trogon." *Animalia*, n.d., animalia.bio. Accessed 6 Dec. 2024.
7. "Cuban Solenodon." *Animalia*, n.d., animalia.bio. Accessed 6 Dec. 2024.
8. "Cuba Wildlife Facts." *PBS*, 1 Apr. 2020, pbs.org. Accessed 6 Dec. 2024.
9. Bryn Nelson. "Exploring the Mysteries of Cuba's Coral Reefs." *Science News Explores*, 15 Mar. 2018, snexplores.org. Accessed 6 Dec. 2024.
10. "Cuban Crocodile." *Smithsonian's National Zoo & Conservation Biology Institute*, n.d., nationalzoo.si.edu. Accessed 6 Dec. 2024.
11. Heinz Fritz Wermuth and James P. Ross. "Crocodile." *Britannica*, 30 Oct. 2024, britannica.com. Accessed 6 Dec. 2024.
12. "The World's Smallest Frog." *Endangered Species International*, 2011, endangeredspeciesinternational.org. Accessed 6 Dec. 2024.
13. "Cuba Wildlife Facts."

CHAPTER 4. HISTORY

1. Franklin W. Knight and Sandra H. Levinson. "Soils of Cuba." *Britannica*, 5 Dec. 2024, britannica.com. Accessed 6 Dec. 2024.
2. Martin A. Tsang. "Chinese Influences on Life and Religion in Cuba." *University of Miami News*, 2023, cuba.miami.edu. Accessed 6 Dec. 2024.
3. "Early Cuba–1868: Colonialism, International Sugar Trade and the Development of Nationalism." *Cuba Unbound*, 2024, cubaunbound.com. Accessed 6 Dec. 2024.
4. Knight and Levinson, "Soils of Cuba."
5. B. Denise Hawkins. "In Cuba, African Roots Run Deep, but It's a Lesson Students Aren't Learning in the Classroom." *NBC News*, 1 Sept. 2017, nbcnews.com. Accessed 6 Dec. 2024.
6. "Cuban Independence Movement." *Britannica*, 3 Dec. 2024, britannica.com. Accessed 6 Dec. 2024.

SOURCE NOTES CONTINUED

CHAPTER 5. PEOPLE AND CULTURE

1. "Cuba Population." *Worldometer*, 1 July 2023, worldometers.info. Accessed 6 Dec. 2024.
2. Nora Gámez Torres. "Cuba Admits to Massive Emigration Wave: A Million People Left in Two Years amid Crisis." *Miami Herald*, 24 July 2024, miamiherald.com. Accessed 6 Dec. 2024.
3. "Life Expectancy at Birth, Total (Years)—World." *World Bank Group*, 2024, data.worldbank.org. Accessed 6 Dec. 2024.
4. "Cuba Demographics." *Worldometer*, 2024, worldometers.info. Accessed 6 Dec. 2024.
5. "Cuba Demographics."
6. "Edificio Bacardí." *Lonely Planet*, 2025, lonelyplanet.com. Accessed 6 Dec. 2024.
7. Gabe Wood. "How Many People Speak Spanish? A Full Breakdown by Country." *Rosetta Stone*, 9 May 2024, blog.rosettastone.com. Accessed 6 Dec. 2024.
8. Nick Moroff. "After 50 Years, Cuba Says Its Baseball Players Can Go Abroad." *NPR*, 28 Nov. 2013, npr.org. Accessed 6 Dec. 2024.
9. Robert Huish. "Cuba's Olympic Delegation Is the Smallest in Decades—and It Reveals the Country's Socioeconomic Crisis." *Conversation*, 19 July 2024, theconversation.com. Accessed 6 Dec. 2024.
10. "2022 Report on International Religious Freedom: Cuba." *US Department of State*, 30 Nov. 2022, state.gov. Accessed 6 Dec. 2024.
11. Jay Jaffe. "Rays' Exhibition Game in Cuba Brings Two Countries Closer." *Sports Illustrated*, 22 Mar. 2016, si.com. Accessed 6 Dec. 2024.

CHAPTER 6. POLITICS

1. "Republic of Cuba." *ElectionGuide*, 26 Mar. 2023, electionguide.org. Accessed 14 Jan. 2025.
2. "Cuba." *GlobalSecurity.org*, 2024, globalsecurity.org. Accessed 6 Dec. 2024.
3. "Cuba."

CHAPTER 7. ECONOMICS
1. "What Are the Major Natural Resources of Cuba?" *World Atlas*, n.d., worldatlas.com. Accessed 6 Dec. 2024.
2. Ed Augustin. "How Cuba's Sugar Industry Has Been Ground into Dust." *Al Jazeera*, 12 May 2023, aljazeera.com. Accessed 6 Dec. 2024.
3. Franklin W. Knight and Sandra H. Levinson. "Trade of Cuba." *Britannica*, 5 Dec. 2024, britannica.com. Accessed 6 Dec. 2024.
4. "What Are the Major Natural Resources of Cuba?"
5. Nelson Acosta and Marc Frank. "Cubans Struggle as Peso Loses Half Its Value in a Year on Informal Market." *Reuters*, 2 Aug. 2023, reuters.com. Accessed 6 Dec. 2024.
6. "Aging Cuban Infrastructure Means Water Shortages for Havana." *Al Jazeera*, 4 July 2023, aljazeera.com. Accessed 6 Dec. 2024.
7. Diana Rita Cabrera. "How to Get Around in Cuba: Classic Cars, Coaches and Carriages." *Lonely Planet*, 8 Jan. 2023, lonelyplanet.com. Accessed 6 Dec. 2024.

CHAPTER 8. CUBA TODAY
1. "Cuba Tourism Statistics—October 31, 2023." *Cuba Business Report*, 13 Dec. 2023, cubabusinessreport.com. Accessed 6 Dec. 2024.
2. "University of Havana." *Times Higher Education*, 2024, timeshighereducation.com. Accessed 6 Dec. 2024.
3. "Literacy Rate of People Ages 15 Years and Over in Cuba from 1981 to 2021." *Statista*, 5 Dec. 2024, statista.com. Accessed 6 Dec. 2024.
4. Carla Gloria Colomé. "'The Great Medical Powerhouse Has No Doctors': Parents of Sick Children Denounce the Health Crisis in Cuba." *País*, 23 Oct. 2023, english.elpais.com. Accessed 6 Dec. 2024.
5. "Cuba: Events of 2022." *Human Rights Watch World Report*, 2022, hrw.org. Accessed 6 Dec. 2024.
6. "Five Things You Should Know a Year On from Cuba's 11 July Protests." *Amnesty International*, 11 July 2022, amnesty.org. Accessed 6 Dec. 2024.

INDEX

antique cars, 11, 86, 89
architecture, 20, 55–56, 86
Arnaz, Desi, 60

baseball, 62–65, 94
Batista, Fulgencio, 47–48, 60
bee hummingbirds, 32

Carnival of Santiago de Cuba, 13, 66
Castro, Fidel, 13, 47, 48, 50, 64, 65, 66, 79, 92
Castro, Raúl, 50–51, 74
Cathedral of Havana, 8, 55
Catholicism, 65–66, 69
Cauto River, 16, 21–22
caves, 21
Ciboney people, 38
climate, 22–25, 26, 29, 33, 41
coffee, 13, 20, 41, 57, 80
Cold War, 48–50
Columbus, Christopher, 40, 41
communism, 48, 65, 70–73
coral reefs, 18, 33–35
COVID-19 pandemic, 98

CubaMessenger, 6
Cuban crocodiles, 35–36
Cuban Missile Crisis, 48–50
Cuban Revolution, 10, 44–48, 74
Cuban royal palms, 29–30
Cuban trogons, 31–32
Cuban War of Independence, 43
currency, 83–85

dance, 13, 62, 99
Díaz-Canel, Miguel, 51, 74, 79, 85, 98
dominoes, 64

Edificio Bacardí, 56
education, 73, 74, 92–94
English language, 7
Escambray Mountains, 20–21
Estrada Palma, Tomás, 44

farming, 80
Fast & Furious, 6, 11
Figueredo, Pedro, 77
fishing, 35, 78, 80–82

food, 6, 7, 12, 13, 17, 51, 57–59, 61, 65, 82, 85, 94, 97, 99
Franqui, Carlos, 50
freedom of expression, 97–98
freedom of speech, 75
freedom of the press, 73

gardening, 94
government, 7, 8, 42–43, 44, 47–48, 51, 60, 64, 65, 70, 73, 75–76, 78, 85, 86, 89, 92, 93, 96, 97–98
Gran Piedra, La, 16, 18–20
Guamuhaya Mountains, 21
Guanahatabey people, 38, 40
Guevara, Che, 10

holidays, 66–69
Hurricane Ian, 25
Hurricane Irma, 25
Hurricane Milton, 25

infrastructure, 86–89
Isla de la Juventud, 14–17, 36

CHAPTER 7. ECONOMICS

1. "What Are the Major Natural Resources of Cuba?" *World Atlas*, n.d., worldatlas.com. Accessed 6 Dec. 2024.
2. Ed Augustin. "How Cuba's Sugar Industry Has Been Ground into Dust." *Al Jazeera*, 12 May 2023, aljazeera.com. Accessed 6 Dec. 2024.
3. Franklin W. Knight and Sandra H. Levinson. "Trade of Cuba." *Britannica*, 5 Dec. 2024, britannica.com. Accessed 6 Dec. 2024.
4. "What Are the Major Natural Resources of Cuba?"
5. Nelson Acosta and Marc Frank. "Cubans Struggle as Peso Loses Half Its Value in a Year on Informal Market." *Reuters*, 2 Aug. 2023, reuters.com. Accessed 6 Dec. 2024.
6. "Aging Cuban Infrastructure Means Water Shortages for Havana." *Al Jazeera*, 4 July 2023, aljazeera.com. Accessed 6 Dec. 2024.
7. Diana Rita Cabrera. "How to Get Around in Cuba: Classic Cars, Coaches and Carriages." *Lonely Planet*, 8 Jan. 2023, lonelyplanet.com. Accessed 6 Dec. 2024.

CHAPTER 8. CUBA TODAY

1. "Cuba Tourism Statistics—October 31, 2023." *Cuba Business Report*, 13 Dec. 2023, cubabusinessreport.com. Accessed 6 Dec. 2024.
2. "University of Havana." *Times Higher Education*, 2024, timeshighereducation.com. Accessed 6 Dec. 2024.
3. "Literacy Rate of People Ages 15 Years and Over in Cuba from 1981 to 2021." *Statista*, 5 Dec. 2024, statista.com. Accessed 6 Dec. 2024.
4. Carla Gloria Colomé. "'The Great Medical Powerhouse Has No Doctors': Parents of Sick Children Denounce the Health Crisis in Cuba." *País*, 23 Oct. 2023, english.elpais.com. Accessed 6 Dec. 2024.
5. "Cuba: Events of 2022." *Human Rights Watch World Report*, 2022, hrw.org. Accessed 6 Dec. 2024.
6. "Five Things You Should Know a Year On from Cuba's 11 July Protests." *Amnesty International*, 11 July 2022, amnesty.org. Accessed 6 Dec. 2024.

INDEX

antique cars, 11, 86, 89
architecture, 20, 55–56, 86
Arnaz, Desi, 60

baseball, 62–65, 94
Batista, Fulgencio, 47–48, 60
bee hummingbirds, 32

Carnival of Santiago de Cuba, 13, 66
Castro, Fidel, 13, 47, 48, 50, 64, 65, 66, 79, 92
Castro, Raúl, 50–51, 74
Cathedral of Havana, 8, 55
Catholicism, 65–66, 69
Cauto River, 16, 21–22
caves, 21
Ciboney people, 38
climate, 22–25, 26, 29, 33, 41
coffee, 13, 20, 41, 57, 80
Cold War, 48–50
Columbus, Christopher, 40, 41
communism, 48, 65, 70–73
coral reefs, 18, 33–35
COVID-19 pandemic, 98

CubaMessenger, 6
Cuban crocodiles, 35–36
Cuban Missile Crisis, 48–50
Cuban Revolution, 10, 44–48, 74
Cuban royal palms, 29–30
Cuban trogons, 31–32
Cuban War of Independence, 43
currency, 83–85

dance, 13, 62, 99
Díaz-Canel, Miguel, 51, 74, 79, 85, 98
dominoes, 64

Edificio Bacardí, 56
education, 73, 74, 92–94
English language, 7
Escambray Mountains, 20–21
Estrada Palma, Tomás, 44

farming, 80
Fast & Furious, 6, 11
Figueredo, Pedro, 77
fishing, 35, 78, 80–82

food, 6, 7, 12, 13, 17, 51, 57–59, 61, 65, 82, 85, 94, 97, 99
Franqui, Carlos, 50
freedom of expression, 97–98
freedom of speech, 75
freedom of the press, 73

gardening, 94
government, 7, 8, 42–43, 44, 47–48, 51, 60, 64, 65, 70, 73, 75–76, 78, 85, 86, 89, 92, 93, 96, 97–98
Gran Piedra, La, 16, 18–20
Guamuhaya Mountains, 21
Guanahatabey people, 38, 40
Guevara, Che, 10

holidays, 66–69
Hurricane Ian, 25
Hurricane Irma, 25
Hurricane Milton, 25

infrastructure, 86–89
Isla de la Juventud, 14–17, 36

Kennedy, John F., 50
Khrushchev, Nikita, 50

languages, 4, 56–57, 93
López, Narciso, 77

Manuel de Céspedes, Carlos, 8, 42
Martí, José, 4, 6, 42
medical care shortages, 96–97
military, 4, 44, 49, 76, 78–79
Monte Iberia eleuths, 36
Museo del Automóvil, 10–11
music, 9–10, 13, 61–62, 66, 93, 99

natural resources, 80, 82–83

Old Havana, 7–10, 55, 86, 89

pharmaceutical industry, 83
Pico San Juan, 16, 21
Pico Turquino, 18
Pinar del Río province, 25, 38
Platt Amendment, 44
Plaza de Armas, 8

Plaza de la Catedral, 9
population, 13, 40, 52, 55, 59, 65, 86
power outages, 51, 89
protests, 51, 98

ropa vieja, 7, 8, 12

Sierra de Sancti Spíritus, 21
Sierra Maestra, 18, 20
slavery, 41–43
solenodons, 32–33
son Cubano, 9–10, 62
Spanish-American War, 44
Spanish colonization, 40–44
sugar, 41, 42, 44, 57, 59, 80, 82

Taíno people, 38–40, 56
Templete, El, 55–56
Ten Years' War, 42–43
Teurbe Tolón, Emilia, 76
Teurbe Tolón, Miguel, 76
Toa River, 22
tourism, 13, 85, 86, 92
travel, 13, 22, 89, 92

United Nations Educational, Scientific and Cultural Organization (UNESCO), 17, 20, 86
University of Havana, 47, 93

Velázquez de Cuéllar, Diego, 40–41

water shortages, 86–89
Weyler y Nicolau, Valeriano, 44
white mariposa, 26–29
World Heritage sites, 20, 86

Yumurí River, 22

ABOUT THE AUTHOR

TAMMY GAGNE

Tammy Gagne is an author and editor with a passion for educational nonfiction. She has written hundreds of books for both adults and children. Residing in the beautiful state of Maine, she enjoys life with her husband, their son, and two rescue dogs. When not writing or editing, she is often brainstorming her next project. Some of her recent titles are about refugee and immigrant rights and natural disasters such as hurricanes. She hopes they inspire and educate readers of all ages.